Self
(Don't)
Care

200 Ways to Enjoy Life

Without Giving a F*ck

ADAMS MEDIA

NEW YORK LONDON TORONTO SYDNEY NEW DELHI

Adams Media
An Imprint of Simon & Schuster, Inc.
57 Littlefield Street
Avon, Massachusetts 02322

First Adams Media hardcover edition January 2019

ADAMS MEDIA and colophon are trademarks of Simon & Schuster.

For information about special discounts for bulk purchases, please contact Simon & Schuster Special Sales at 1-866-506-1949 or business@simonandschuster.com.

The Simon & Schuster Speakers Bureau can bring authors to your live event. For more information or to book an event contact the Simon & Schuster Speakers Bureau at 1-866-248-3049 or visit our website at www.simonspeakers.com.

Interior design by Sylvia McArdle

Manufactured in the United States of America

10 9 8 7 6 5 4 3 2

Library of Congress Cataloging-in-Publication Data has been applied for.

ISBN 978-1-72140-025-6
ISBN 978-1-72140-026-3 (ebook)

Contains material adapted from the following title published by Adams Media, an Imprint of Simon & Schuster, Inc.: *A Year of Living Sinfully* by Eric Grzymkowski, copyright © 2012, ISBN 978-1-4405-1253-7.

Contents

Introduction

Practice yoga.

Pour yourself a cup of peppermint tea.

Write in your gratitude journal...about how thankful you are for this *boring-ass life*.

Seriously.

What's the point of self-care if you can't actually enjoy yourself? It's time to be selfish about your self-care and do the things you actually care to do. Forget stretching into child's pose, and focus on stretching for the remote from the comfort of your couch. Replace the cup of tea with a bottle of wine, or a bottle of beer, or, better yet, both. And don't bother writing in some journal; instead, write off work for the day and live it up.

With the ideas included in this book, you'll be able to do exactly that. There are 200 suggestions on how to do you—however you damn well please (effects on your body TBD). It's the self-care you need and deserve.

So, let's turn your #selfcaresunday into a Sunday Funday and *actually* live your best life.

Lounge in a Hammock All Day

*"How beautiful it is to do nothing,
and then rest afterward."*
—Spanish Proverb

The mention of a hammock evokes images of swaying palm trees, cool island breezes, and endless piña coladas. Too bad you're stuck in a wintry wonderland. But luckily hammocks needn't be limited to faraway tropical paradises; the sun doesn't have to be shining in order for you to lounge around all day.

Once you've procured your hammock, get busy doing nothing. Place a stack of magazines and books within reach, along with a cooler full of lemonade, beer, or fruity cocktail creations. If you're just content to lie there free of distractions, go ahead and let the soft swaying of your suspended bed lull you into a deep relaxing sleep.

You may have a lot to do today, but is any of that stuff as appealing as taking a tropical vacation in your living room?

PRO TIP

Go for a fabric hammock
if you have a choice.
The knots on traditional rope
hammocks can leave uncom-
fortable marks on the skin.

Throw a BYOE
(Bring Your Own Everything) Party

"After all, what is your host's purpose in having a party?
Surely not for you to enjoy yourself; if that were their
sole purpose, they'd have simply sent champagne
and women over to your place by taxi."
—P.J. O'Rourke, humorist

Take the idea of a potluck to the next level and outsource everything you need for a party to your guests. Don't just limit your guests to the typical six-pack and a bag of chips. You're providing the most important thing— the location—so it's only fair that your friends pull their own weight. Keep a master list of everything you'll need. Things like cups and soda are expected, but what about those necessary items like toilet paper and dish detergent? Each time a guest asks if he can bring something, say "Yes" and assign him one of the items. Don't be afraid to include some things you've been needing around the house too. If guests seem confused when you ask them to bring cat food, just respond, "It's gonna be one hell of a party."

PRO TIP

Always establish a designated driver or make a plan for taking a cab home so no one is drinking and driving.

PARTY MUST-HAVES

- Alcohol
- Music
- Snacks
- Bottle opener
- Party game

Drive 100 MPH

"Remember, folks, stoplights timed for 35 mph are also timed for 70 mph."
—Jim Samuels, comedian

For the most part nobody adheres to speed limits. Traveling five to ten miles per hour over is pretty much standard. But for some reason we all stop there. Everyone has the urge to gun it and let her rip now and then, yet we never indulge that urge.

Sure, it's dangerous, and you have to pay a fine if you get caught, but so what? Live a little. Besides, you'll be a safer driver once you know what your car is really capable of.

Find a long stretch of highway and do a preliminary pass, keeping an eye out for speed traps. Once you are sure the coast is clear, double back and get ready for your speed run. Open the windows and feel the rush of air as you hit 100 mph and zoom past hordes of law-abiding motorists. Once you've enjoyed the rush of adrenaline for a bit, ease back down to a reasonable speed before Smokey gets on your tail.

PRO TIP

Turn off your cell phone to avoid distracting text messages or calls.

FASTEST CAR

In August 2018, Danny Thompson drove the Challenger II, a car built by his father fifty years previously, across Utah's Bonneville Salt Flats, beating the wheel-driven land speed record. Thompson reached the stunning speed of 448 mph.

Ignore Oral Hygiene

"I told my dentist my teeth are going yellow.
He told me to wear a brown tie."
—Rodney Dangerfield, comedian

When you were a kid, brushing your teeth seemed like the vilest of punishments, second only to taking a bath or cleaning your room. This part of your daily routine may not seem so terrible as an adult, but maybe your childhood self was onto something.

If you stopped worrying about your teeth, you could chow down on cotton candy, soda, and ice cream to your heart's content. Think of all the real estate you'd free up in your pockets by ditching breath mints and chewing gum. Our ancestors lived without toothpaste for centuries. You can live without it for twenty-four hours.

So leave your floss next to the sink for the day, and resist the urge to pick up a toothbrush. Get creative and gargle with soda instead of mouthwash or floss with licorice rope. Sure, it may be gross, but thankfully your family and friends are the ones who have to deal with your dragon breath, not you.

ALTERNATIVE BREATH FRESHENERS

- Cardamom seeds
- Hydrogen peroxide and water
- Parsley leaves
- Cinnamon sticks
- Baking soda

PRO TIP

Don't bathe either. The smell may mask your daylong morning breath.

Tell Off Your Boss by Anonymous Email

"Accomplishing the impossible means only that the boss will add it to your regular duties."

—Doug Larson, journalist

Your boss is kind of a jerk sometimes. Your boss makes you do work, corrects your so-called mistakes, makes more money than you do, and sits in a bigger office. What a jerk. You tell people about it over drinks after work and with your friends at dinner. But it's high time you tell your boss directly.

Of course you don't have the cojones or the financial capital to afford that. The obvious solution is to send an anonymous email. Set up a fake email account that wouldn't ever be linked to you, write out everything you ever wanted to tell your boss, and edit it for expletives. If you don't do it, your boss will never stop being a jerk. He'll never correct his little habit of clicking his cheek when he's done asking you for a favor. And he'll never stop leaning back in his chair with his legs crossed like a smug jerk. So do the courageous thing: anonymously send an email detailing all your boss's shortcomings. You'll be an office hero, even if no one can ever know it.

PRO TIP

Use a public computer for
everything so the
IP address can't be traced
back to you.

Consume an Entire Pizza by Yourself

*"You better cut the pizza in four pieces because
I'm not hungry enough to eat six."*
—Yogi Berra, baseball player

With a telephone and a few extra dollars, anyone can enjoy the wonder that is the cheesy, gooey American pizza. But just because you don't have a party going on in your house doesn't mean you shouldn't go for the whole pie. After all, you're hungry—and you don't have to be.

Of course, a more practical person might order the deliverable minimum, eat a small portion, and save the rest for later. But leftover pizza simply isn't the same as a hot, oven-fresh pie. Besides, you can always hit the gym and make up for your evening of gluttony some other time.

Since this pizza is for you and you alone, feel free to go nuts. Get every topping on the menu and even some that aren't. And don't even think about blotting it with a napkin first. The greasier, the better.

DRINKS THAT GO WELL WITH PIZZA

- $200 Cabernet Sauvignon
- Johnnie Walker Blue
- Imported oak-aged pilsner retailing at $20 per bottle

PRO TIP

Avoid all food but nuts and berries for twelve hours prior to the pizza binge. You want your stomach to be empty, but not so empty that it shrinks.

Selectively Obey
Traffic Laws

"I believe in rules. Sure I do. If there weren't any rules,
how could you break them?"
—Leo Durocher, baseball coach

Bicyclists have it good. When they want to move fast, they can take up the entire lane and act like a car. But the moment there's a red light, they just zoom on through and nobody gives them a second glance. Their rampant disregard for certain traffic laws may be illegal, but it's certainly enticing. Imagine how much less stressful your commute would be if you could pick and choose which laws you follow.

When you drive around today, use your judgment when it comes to the rules of the road. If you're the only person on the highway, perhaps you shouldn't bother hitting your turn signal. If there's nobody approaching at a four-way stop, it's safe to assume you can roll through without coming to a complete stop.

You are a busy person with places to go and people to see. If bending a few rules gets you on your way a little faster, perhaps it's worth the risk of a ticket.

PRO TIP

Space your violations a
few miles apart. If you get
stopped, you don't want the
cop to string several
tickets together.

Order Delivery from the Closest Restaurant

"You don't need a silver fork to eat good food."
—Paul Prudhomme, chef

More likely than not, you have a go-to restaurant for those times where you want a delicious fresh-cooked meal but don't have the energy to turn on the oven. But what about when you are not only too lazy to cook, but you're also too lazy to even make it out the door? Sure, a pizzeria or Chinese restaurant will deliver right to your door, but you shouldn't have to settle for greasy pizza or gloppy mystery meat. You may be lazy, but you're not broke.

Call up your restaurant of choice and ask if you can reserve a table for one. Then politely request that the staff set up that table in a special location: your living room. Before the person hangs up on you, insist that you will make it worth the waiter's while. Offer to pay double or even triple the menu price, and promise a generous tip on top. You may meet with some resistance at first, but the restaurant should eventually cave to the power of the almighty dollar.

PRO TIP

Answer the door carrying crutches to justify the 100-foot delivery request.

WORLD'S LONGEST PIZZA DELIVERY

In 2006 Paul Fenech traveled 12,347 miles to hand-deliver a pizza from Opera Pizza in Madrid, Spain, to a customer in Wellington, New Zealand.

Hog the Bathroom

"How long a minute is depends on what side of the bathroom door you're on."
—Unknown

At first glance there really isn't much to enjoy about your morning routine—especially when it is interrupted every five minutes by an impatient spouse or roommate eager for a turn. But you'd be surprised how much more pleasant it can be when you simply ignore the irritated bangs on the door and enjoy yourself.

Instead of rushing through your shower to preserve hot water, crank it up as high as it will go and bask in the warmth. Since you've gotten the bathroom nice and steamy, now might be the ideal time to lounge around in your towel and catch up on some reading. At the very least it's a chance to mentally prepare yourself for the day ahead.

Sure, your partner may be a little peeved after the first half hour or so, but that's a small price to pay for your own personal day spa. If the whining becomes too much of a nuisance, you can always drown it out by singing in the shower. The more irritating the tune, the better.

PRO TIP

Check the locks beforehand to prevent unwanted intrusion.

VIABLE EXCUSES

- "I forgot how to turn the shower off."
- "Aliens abducted me for an hour."
- "I didn't know I couldn't do that."

Sample Every Ice Cream Flavor

"Ice cream is happiness condensed."
—Jessi Lane Adams, writer

Unless you live next door to a Baskin-Robbins, you're probably stuck satisfying your evening sweet tooth with a leftover, half-eaten carton of ice cream. And let's be honest: freezer burn isn't all that satisfying. The next time your sweet tooth strikes, don't settle for anything less than all thirty-one flavors—and do it without paying for a single scoop.

Instead of politely nibbling one flavor and then ordering a scoop, ask for another sample. After all, you can't be expected to choose if you don't know all of your options. Just feign uncertainty and work your way through the freezer case. You'll know you're finished when you have a fistful of tiny plastic spoons and a sugar rush to rival that of any six-year-old in town. Throw a buck in the tip jar, and head back home to sleep the sweetest of dreams.

PRO TIP

It's tempting to order willy-nilly and shout out flavors as they come to mind, but it pays to be methodical. Working left to right ensures that you hit all the flavors, but a zigzag approach prevents the staff from catching on right away.

AMERICA'S FAVORITE FLAVORS

- Vanilla
- Chocolate
- Butter pecan
- Strawberry
- Mint chocolate chip

Lie about Your Age

"Age is something that doesn't matter, unless you are a cheese."
—Billie Burke, actress

You know what's fun? Being young. You get to do stupid things, make mistakes freely, and have a great body and a wrinkle-free face to boot. And while aging has its upsides—hello, acquired wisdom and legally available alcohol!—the grass will always seem greener on the younger side.

Fortunately it's no one's business how old you are. So lie about it. If you're on the far side of thirty, hop back over that fence and be twenty-four again. Hit the bars in your favorite mid-twenties ensemble (tube tops for the ladies and button-down shirts for the men are still popular choices). Dance the night away in the club with some sweaty dude wearing Axe body spray. Find a local frat party and do a few keg stands. Flirt blatantly with the twenty-three-year-old barista at your local Starbucks. If anyone asks (but why would they?), claim to be sticking within your age range. After all, you're only as old as you feel. And if you're feeling twenty-two tonight, by all means, go shotgun some beers.

PRO TIP

Make sure to keep your driver's license hidden at all times.

THE EYES HAVE IT

You can't judge a person's age by her eyeballs. Why? A human's eyes stay roughly the same size from infancy to old age.

Bum a Ride Off Your Bud

"A true friend is someone who thinks that you are a good egg even though he knows that you are slightly cracked."
—Bernard Meltzer, radio host

Though most people can drive, not everyone likes doing it. It's hard finding pleasure in coasting along the same route to work, home, and the grocery store. In fact it can be so "pleasureless" that using deception to get out of driving feels rather shameless.

The next time you plan on driving to meet your pals, force them to come get you. You deserve a break, and it wouldn't hurt to save a little gas. Tell your pals that your car is in the shop and that your bike just won't cut it. Make sure to park your vehicle up the street so your friends won't see it when they pick you up.

If your friends give you any trouble, promise to pick them up next time. Buy them a drink or two, but make sure they don't overdo it. They are your automatic designated drivers tonight, after all.

PRO TIP

Make sure to come up with a "car problem" to bitch about at the bar. It will make your situation more believable.

VIABLE CAR ISSUES

- "The starter died."
- "I forgot to get the oil changed."
- "The A/C won't work and it's hot out, bro."

Skip Out on Dinner with the In-Laws

"Just got back from a pleasure trip:
I took my mother-in-law to the airport."
—Henny Youngman, comedian

As if one overbearing set of parents wasn't enough, tradition sees fit to slap us with a fresh new pair the moment we get married. Best of all, unlike your adoring parents, this new set doesn't even like you. In all likelihood they downright hate you.

Yet, despite their unbridled disdain for you, they invite you over for dinner every Sunday. You bit the bullet and have put up with their incessant nagging and general disappointment for years. Enough is enough. Tonight you are going to do what you've always dreamed but never dared to do: just say no. Forget the excuses and don't bother faking sick; just don't go. Sure, your spouse will want to murder you, but at least you won't have to sit through another slideshow of your in-laws' Alaska cruise.

Since you have the evening to yourself, make a relaxing dinner for one, pour yourself an expensive glass of wine, and toast to the first night of an in-law-free existence.

PRO TIP

Get a blanket and a pillow, and set them up on the couch. Because that's where you'll be sleeping tonight.

Fart in a Crowded Elevator

"I did not win the Nobel Fart Prize."

—*Bart Simpson,* The Simpsons

Like real estate, farting is all about one thing: location, location, location. Whether you're in the privacy of your own home or in a public space among strangers matters greatly in how your fart will be received. Still, bystanders remain mostly powerless against olfactory offenses—which is why the next time you're stuck in a crowded elevator and have to let one rip, have at it.

The elevator is a perfect spot to fart because other people are trapped. They have nowhere to go, and the air is creeping closer and closer to them. Lucky for you, your own fart smell is good, so it's not a problem. Some people may put their noses in their shirts or make a comment, but you just keep smiling away like you're skipping in the sun. As one final act of war against your elevator mates, if people raise a fuss with you, silently point your thumb at the guy to your right.

PRO TIP

Don't do this after having a spicy bean burrito.

OTHER RUDE THINGS TO DO IN A CROWDED ELEVATOR

- Talk on your cell phone
- Stretch
- Sneeze
- Jog in place
- Projectile-vomit
- Sweat profusely

Eat Only Things Containing Chocolate

"What you see before you, my friend,
is the result of a lifetime of chocolate."
—Katharine Hepburn, actress

Since you likely eat at least three times a day, it's important to do it with style, class, and grace. It's also important to eat things that are really delicious.

If there's one thing uniting the world, it's our unending love affair with chocolate. So play your own game of Iron Chef for the day, and make chocolate the secret ingredient. It's decadent. It's delicious. And some dark chocolate is good for you. Studies have even shown that eating a small bar every day can lower both blood pressure and cholesterol. So, logically, eating the equivalent of 100 small bars must be 100 times better for you.

In the morning you can start with a breakfast of chocolate cereal with chocolate milk. Then, instead of your regular morning coffee, order a mocha latte. For lunch have a Nutella sandwich. As for dinner, devour an entire chocolate cake. When you have your sugar hangover later that night, take two Advil and wash it down with a nice cup of hot cocoa. Rules are rules.

PRO TIP

Brush your teeth a few extra
times during the day.

Buy Only Junk Food at the Supermarket

"My body is a temple where junk food goes to worship."
—Unknown

Your grocery list is starting to look like the ingredient list for your dog's all-natural organic kibble. Free-range, locally raised chicken breasts. Kale and chard. Brown rice and lentils. No, you wouldn't dream of buying a bag of potato chips! Not that they're not good, but…come to think of it, potato chips are really frickin' good.

So just this once, hit the local supermarket—not Whole Foods, not Trader Joe's, but the regular supermarket. Skip the perimeter (that's where they keep all the healthy stuff) and go straight for the aisles. Then fill your basket with the worst of it: greasy potato chips, neon cheese balls, chemically created baked goods, ice cream in a tub, cheese in a can, cookies in a tube. Does it get any more wicked than this?

When you get home, go at it. Eat the cookie dough straight from the tube. Get cheese dust all over your fingers and syrupy chocolate sauce under your fingernails. Eat until you feel like you might vomit. Tomorrow morning you can hit the reset button—and kale may have never tasted so good.

PRO TIP

Be sure to throw out those potato chip bags and Twinkie wrappers once you're done binging. People might judge.

Jump Into Leaf Piles

"Autumn is a second spring when every leaf is a flower."
—Albert Camus, French philosopher

One of the things you don't find out in homeowner school is that you will spend most of your fall weekends removing dead foliage from your lawn and organizing it into neat little piles. You also didn't learn that it is impossible to shake the childhood urge to dive headfirst into said piles. If only there were a way to indulge that desire without negating all that hard work.

Well, you're not the only one with trees in the area. Surely your neighbors have equally inviting leaf piles in which you can play. It seems their piles aren't nearly as orderly as your own. If anything you'll be doing them a favor by scattering the leaves again. Clearly they could use the practice. Check around for witnesses before performing a cannonball right into your neighbor's pile. Take some time to revel in the leafy goodness: construct a leaf hat, build a leaf fort, fall backward and make leaf angels. Once you've had your fill, hightail it out of there before anyone catches on and hands you a rake.

PRO TIP

Wash your clothes immediately to remove incriminating leaf residue.

DANGERS TO WATCH OUT FOR

- Animal "leavings"
- Jagged rake tines
- Broken bottles

Slide Down the Banister

*"As you slide down the banister of life,
may the splinters never point the wrong way."*
—*Old Irish Blessing*

Bart Simpson was hardly the first fictional character to slide down the banister, but he certainly made it fashionable and opened the practice up to a wider audience. But instead of ending your journey with a loud offscreen thud like Bart, a successful slide down the banister ends like a gymnastics routine—with a graceful landing. That's why it's important to not be carrying bulky, cumbersome items while sliding. They could compromise the entire endeavor.

There are any number of reasons to slide down the banister. In this modern world where time is a luxury, sliding down the banister is a quicker way to get from point A to point B. Maybe there's a subway train about to depart that you need to catch. Or perhaps you're running from a predator. Maybe you don't want to touch the disease-ridden banister with the same hands you feed yourself with. Or maybe you're just trying to impress a passing stranger. In any case it's a great way to travel in style. And it's damn fun.

PRO TIP

Before you decide to slide, make sure the banister ends with a smooth curve down and not with a pointy knob or engraved figurine.

Cheat at Trivia Night

"Why is it trivia? People call it trivia because they know nothing and they are embarrassed about it."

—Robbie Coltrane, actor

Everyone loves the excitement of Trivia Night—until their team loses week after week after week. Surely the opposing teams can't really know off the top of their head what color George Washington's eyes were or what the capital of Namibia is. They must be cheating!

Maybe they are and maybe they aren't, but obviously there is only one way for you to win a damn Trivia Night—whip out the smartphone. Yes, it's against the rules, but it's Trivia Night, not the Olympic figure skating competition.

You probably don't want to get everything right on the night you "win"—be sure to leave one or two wrong answers. Above all, be discreet so no one else will be the wiser. But if you do get caught, just laugh it off and find a new Trivia Night—after all, a slap on the wrist is a small price to pay for self-esteem.

PRO TIP

Choose a table in a dark corner of the bar to decrease the chances of getting caught.

BEST TRIVIA WEBSITES

- www.sporcle.com
- www.funtrivia.com
- www.factacular.com

BYOB to a Bar

"A bartender is just a pharmacist
with limited inventory."
—*Unknown*

Bars can be great places to unwind and meet new people, but unless you plan to sit and nurse a glass of tap water all night, they're also super-pricey. The average bar charges around a 300 percent markup for drinks, which is hard-earned money out of your pocket every time you take a sip. Luckily there's a simple solution to the problem. Instead of spending your life savings at the neighborhood pub, invest in a flask and BYOB. Is it illegal? Perhaps. Is it frowned upon? Most certainly. But can you get away with it? Definitely.

The bar is packed, so nobody is going to notice if you top off your glass of Coke with a little whiskey. If you're nervous, just play bartender in the bathroom. Let those other suckers squander their money as they wish—you know how to beat the system.

PRO TIP

Keep your pals in the dark about your little secret—otherwise everyone will want in on your hooch.

EASY DRINKS TO MIX DISCREETLY

- Screwdriver
- Gin and tonic
- Rum and Coke

Be Late for Everything

"The trouble with being punctual is that nobody's there to appreciate it."
—Franklin P. Jones, journalist

In our task-oriented society, it seems that punctuality is heralded above all other virtues. But if you stop to think about it, perhaps you spend a little too much time worrying about being on time. Here's a new motto: you'll get there when you get there.

If your friend says, "Meet me for coffee at 2:00," give yourself permission to get there at 2:30. Roll into work at 10:00, and promise to stay late to make up the difference. Skip the apologetic glances when you show up to a movie after the opening credits. Eventually the people around you will adjust. And after all, chances are you'll be a lot happier if you feel free to linger over that cup of coffee instead of just rushing out the door.

PRO TIP

Three exceptions to the rule: job interviews, funerals, weekend visits with your grandmother.

THE EXPECTATION OF LATENESS

In Mexico City locals advise showing up at least an hour late for dinner. A guest who arrives any earlier risks surprising an unprepared host.

Fake a Doctor's Appointment

"Truth is beautiful, without doubt; but so are lies."
—Ralph Waldo Emerson, American philosopher

Everyone fakes being sick every now and then. But what about those times when you don't need the whole day off, just an hour or two? It would be great if you could just tell your boss you need an hour to recharge, but most managers would laugh in your face if you tried that. Enter the fake doctor's appointment. For all the times you've come in early, stayed late, and skipped lunch, you deserve a little time off. It's just a shame you have to pretend to be at the dentist to get it.

Stroll into your boss's office and remind her that you need to duck out to see the doctor. Most bosses will assume you already cleared it with them and they merely forgot. Keep any explanation to a minimum, as you don't want your boss asking too many questions.

Once you are free, get some distance from the office and sneak in some leisure time. Read a book, take a walk, stare at the clouds. Just remember that you bought yourself only an hour or two max. It doesn't take an entire afternoon to get your teeth cleaned.

PRO TIP

Come back sucking on a lollipop with a bandage on your arm to reinforce the lie.

Use Cheats to Beat a Video Game

"Video games are bad for you? That's what they said about rock and roll."
—Shigeru Miyamoto, video game designer

Video games are a potential source of hours of entertainment. They're also a potential source of hours of frustration. Sometimes, despite our best intentions, we just aren't good enough to accomplish something. You may have run into this problem with the castle in the seventh kingdom of *Super Mario Bros. 3*. And the theme music is so ingrained in your head that now you're starting to sing old Beatles songs to the beat.

Luckily for you there is a solution. Just type a cheat into the game. The game's creators wouldn't have put it there if it wasn't supposed to be used. Cheats are as close as a *Google* search away. Up down left right B A B A up…or something. Suddenly you have unlimited lives and automatic flying power. That'll make jumping on the boss's head three times a cinch. Unfortunately there are eight worlds in *Super Mario Bros. 3*, and you have an entire new world of frustration awaiting you.

PRO TIP

Stretch your hand muscles every hour for about ten minutes to avoid carpal tunnel syndrome.

Jump in Puddles

"You can't tell how deep a puddle is until you step into it."
—Unknown

April showers bring May flowers. But they also bring out a bad attitude in everyone and turn the sidewalks into rushing rivers. Instead of spending the month of April glowering under an umbrella or hiding in your damp apartment building, embrace both the weather and your inner child. Go puddle jumping.

You're not supposed to do this past the age of ten, but where's the logic in that? Sure, it looks a little childlike. But if you're trudging through a nor'easter or a spring storm, you're going to end up soaked anyway. You might as well have some fun on your walk. And just try jumping in a puddle without smiling. It's impossible. You'll be loving life as you stomp in one puddle after another, sending rain showers up and onto the unsuspecting passersby power-walking past you.

PRO TIP

Jumping in puddles is a lot like jumping into a leaf pile—it's a childhood activity that's still a lot of fun and virtually injury-free. Shake off your uptight adult fears of stained clothes or soggy shoes, and just have some fun.

PUDDLE-JUMPING PLAYLIST

- "Umbrella," Rihanna
- "Singin' in the Rain," *Singin' in the Rain* movie soundtrack
- "Purple Rain," Prince
- Anything by Taylor Swift or Katy Perry

Dine and Ditch on Your Friends

"Desperate times call for desperate measures."
—Proverb

Dining out with your buds can be quite the bonding experience, but the impending bill may take away your appetite. Sometimes you need to resort to bold measures to save face in tough economic times. The next time you're eating out, pull a fast one. The trick is to pick the perfect moment to up and leave your pals with the check. After ordering several alcoholic drinks and downing half your meal, start fidgeting in your seat. Look nervously at random people in the restaurant, and mumble that you "just gotta go" before launching out of the booth. Your friends will be too confused to notice you never dropped money on the table.

Remember they're your friends! They are allowed to cover your bill for the night. You'd help them out, too, if you weren't so goddamn broke.

PRO TIP

Exit the restaurant discreetly to avoid a nasty look from your waiter.

REASONS YOU SHOULDN'T HAVE TO PAY

- You listen to Mike's stupid stories without complaining
- Lauren has owed you $20 for five years
- You never liked them anyway

Rediscover Prank Calling

"Cell phones are the latest invention in rudeness."
—Terri Guillemets, writer

Cell phones have changed the way we live, bringing the world to our fingertips on their shiny and beautiful screens. It's too bad their caller ID feature made prank calling impossible.

And what a shame it is. Think back to high school and how therapeutic it was to prank-call your best frenemy. Back then you could spend hours lying on your bed with your best friends, thinking up witty questions and then slamming down the rotary phone in a fit of giggles. A few hours later, you'd burned off all the stress from that morning's Algebra II pop quiz and had phone-to-phone contact with the most crush-worthy kid in school.

Well, prank calling isn't impossible. You just need to dial *67 to block your number from appearing. And once you do, you can indulge in the baddest bout of prank calling since 1996. You deserve it. You have more stress now and you need a way to relax. So assemble your closest pals, order up a large pizza, crack open a few beers (after all, you're legal now), and work your way through your contacts list.

PRO TIP

For those who really want to kick it old-school, grab a roll of quarters and seek out the one remaining pay phone in town.

Take a Nap at Work

"No day is so bad it can't be fixed with a nap."
—Carrie P. Snow, comedian

Perhaps it's the low, incessant hum of your aging computer, but something about being in an office can make you feel like you haven't slept in days. You should be finishing up a report, but all you can think of is the down comforter and memory foam mattress waiting for you at home. Rather than fight against your droopy eyes, you might as well embrace the inevitable: you need a nap. Once you've had your beauty rest, you'll be ten times more productive than you were before. If anything, you're doing the company a favor by catching a few winks.

Turn off your computer, grab a roll of paper towels (makeshift pillow), and find a quiet place to curl up for a while. Nothing crazy—just a twenty-minute catnap in the abandoned office on the second floor. Chances are nobody will even notice you are gone, which should say something about the true importance of your job.

PRO TIP

Set an alarm on your phone so you don't sleep through the entire day.

BEST PLACES TO SLEEP

- Under your desk
- Empty conference room
- Janitor's closet
- Parked car

Steal Your Friend's Stories to Make Yourself Sound Cool

"A lie is just the truth waiting to be itself."
—Terri Guillemets, writer

You know that story about your friend's wild night in New Orleans by heart because you've heard him tell it so many times. That big, crazy tale is a crowd-pleaser for sure—so why not make it your own? How about the time you caught the shark during that deep-sea fishing trip in college? That didn't happen to you either? Well, no one needs to know that. The truth is your life is pretty boring these days. You're at work on time every day and your bills are always paid—there's not much happening in the way of adventure. Adopting a few of your friend's stories as your own will give you the excitement you're lacking. Besides, without them you might never get laid.

PRO TIP

To ensure you don't get found out, use the stories only when meeting someone new for the first time. That way, if they hear the story from someone else, they'll assume the second person was the one stealing stories from you.

ANATOMY OF A GOOD STORY

- Look your audience in the eye
- Keep it short and simple
- Gesture with your hands
- Build up to the big climax
- Pause for effect

Pimp Your Ride

"When buying a used car, punch the buttons on the radio.
If all the stations are rock and roll, there's a good chance
the transmission is shot."
—Larry Lujack, disc jockey

What you drive says a lot about you. And your silver four-door Honda sedan with a dent on the side isn't sending the right message. The time has come to pimp your ride.

Never mind that you'll spend thousands of dollars on a car that's probably worth a fraction of that. That's the point. First, of course, you'll need a brand-new interior. Get some decals on the side—some fire coming out of rocket launchers would work well. Of course you need a new speaker system and those subwoofers that make your front two tires bounce up and down like you're in a Dr. Dre video. In addition you'll need high-def TV screens in the backs of the headrests, two PlayStation 4 systems for each TV set, and a home theater system in your trunk. And of course, a popcorn machine for when you're watching movies out of your trunk.

Even if you can't live the pimp life, you can pretend.

PRO TIP

While you're at it, get state-of-the-art airbags, perhaps made of cashmere.

REJECTED "PIMP MY..." IDEAS BEFORE MTV SETTLED ON "PIMP MY RIDE"

• Pimp My Toilet
• Pimp My Family Photo Albums
• Pimp My Pet
• Pimp Eye for the Lame Guy

Eat Frozen Pizza with Your Most Expensive Silverware

"It is impossible to overdo luxury."
—French Proverb

Tucked into the far reaches of your forks and knives drawer lies the fancy silverware for "special occasions." The closest you've actually come to such an occasion is the time your friends came over for the latest HBO finale and you ate dinner around the coffee table. And in the far reaches of your freezer, you happen to have a delicious meat lover's pizza just waiting to be eaten.

Why not bring them both out of hiding?

Create your own special occasion with your favorite frozen entrée. While you warm up the oven, pull out the expensive utensils and give them a quick polish. Lay down a tablecloth with your best professional flick, and light a candle for an extra flourish. For the place setting grab a cloth napkin and arrange the silverware in proper fashion. Once the pizza is cooked to perfection and on the table, you're ready to dig in and eat like a king or queen. Royalty never had it this good.

PRO TIP

To keep the silverware intact for when you finally throw a dinner party, don't forget to hand-wash.

Fill Your Coffee Mug
with Booze

"To alcohol! The cause of, and solution to, all of life's problems."
—Homer Simpson, The Simpsons

Just as you were starting to enjoy your weekend, Monday hits you like a sack of bricks, and the dreary workweek begins anew. All your office provides to help you cope is a pot of instant coffee and the occasional Danish. What you really need is something a little stronger.

You don't want to get plastered on the job, but there's certainly no harm in doctoring up your morning coffee with a dash or two of whiskey. It'll perk you up a lot better than coffee alone and help ease you into the day.

If you don't keep a bottle of spirits at the office for just such occasions, pour a few shots into a water bottle and smuggle it in. Mix in some orange juice, and you have yourself a morning screwdriver. If your coworkers get wise, just offer them a little of your bootleg hooch and swear them to secrecy.

PRO TIP

Carry a pack of gum or mints to mask the smell of booze.

MONDAY FUNDAY RECIPE

1 part gin • 1 part triple sec • 1 part vodka • 6 parts orange juice • Splash of grenadine

Combine ingredients in a small shaker with ice. Shake for several seconds, and pour into an opaque water bottle with a straw (to contain the alcohol smell).

Try on Expensive Jewelry Just for Fun

"I have always felt a gift diamond shines so much better than one you buy for yourself."
—Mae West, actress

Diamonds and emeralds and sapphires and rubies—these are a few of your favorite things. Too bad the most impressive piece in your collection is a big chunk of turquoise you bartered away from a street vendor. Even if your only hope for a lavish piece of jewelry involves convincing a man to get down on one knee, that doesn't mean you can't model some pricey baubles just for fun. So head on down to your favorite jewelry store and tell the staff you're shopping for your sister who looks just like you. Or better yet, tell the truth. Women do it every day.

Then go ahead—try on that ruby-encrusted bracelet, the diamond solitaire earrings, the emerald drop necklace. Revel in it. And then walk away. After you spy the price tags, the selections on the street might not look so bad after all.

PRO TIP

If you do decide to make a purchase, be sure to compare prices at another store. Some experts say buying from the upscale brands in the business could mean paying up to 80 percent more.

MOVIE GEM

The iconic scene from the 1990 film *Pretty Woman*, where Richard Gere snaps the necklace case down on Julia Roberts's fingers, was improvised. Roberts's laughter was her natural reaction.

Go Off Your Diet

"I don't mind that I'm fat. You still get the same money."
—Marlon Brando, actor

Starting a new diet is easy; it's following through with it that's the challenging bit. Whether it's smearing your morning bagel with butter instead of margarine or sneaking a midday candy bar, eventually you are going to backslide. So you might as well go for broke.

Sure, you want to get in shape and lose a few pounds, but that's a problem for another day. Think of the ensuing binge as one last hurrah before you replace your daily breakfast burrito with a granola bar. Instead of counting calories and doing sit-ups, today your focus will be seeing how many M&M's you can fit in your mouth and inventing a meal between breakfast and brunch. Just be sure not to attack your non-diet with the same carefree attitude you used for your real one. If you must eat a salad, make sure it's doused with plenty of creamy dressing and topped with no fewer than four strips of bacon.

PRO TIP

Lock all your granola bars and rice cakes in a drawer, and give the key to a close friend.

FOOL'S GOLD SANDWICH

1 pound of cooked bacon
1 loaf of French bread, sliced down the middle and toasted
1 jar of peanut butter
1 jar of grape jelly
Spoon peanut butter and jelly onto toasted bread, and add bacon.

Buy Every Seat for a Movie

"No, I'm sorry, these are taken. They're in the lobby buying popcorn... what are you doing? These are taken, these are taken!"

—*Elaine Benes,* Seinfeld

You've got the perfect Sunday planned: a trip to the movies to see the latest action flick, complete with popcorn, soda, and candy. Unfortunately your perfect day turns into a perfect nightmare when loud, obnoxious movie patrons talk during the film and rip the plastic off candy boxes every five seconds. Enough already!

Next time you hit the movies, spare yourself the annoyance of other humans and buy up every seat in the theater. You might get a few odd looks at the ticket counter, but at least this way you can enjoy a movie in peace without wanting to throw something at the kid kicking the back of your seat for two hours.

Given the cost of movie tickets these days, you might have to take out a loan to buy more than ten seats. It'll be worth it, though—after all, silence is golden.

PRO TIP

Try out different seats before the movie starts to find the best vantage point for your private viewing.

Take Up Smoking

"A cigarette is the perfect type of a perfect pleasure. It is exquisite, and it leaves one unsatisfied. What more can one want?"
—Oscar Wilde, writer

Smoking used to be the epitome of cool. Now most people would sooner admit they club baby seals for a living than reveal they indulge in the occasional cigarette.

For the most part, the stigma makes sense. Cigarettes smell bad, they turn your teeth yellow, and they cause all sorts of health problems—which will make it all the easier to give up when you take up smoking just for one day.

Grab your coat and follow the clouds of smoke to find the resident chimneys in your building. Most will be happy to let you bum a smoke if you don't want to buy your own pack. Puff away and relax for a bit. You now have an excuse to sneak out of the office for five minutes every hour for the day—which can be far more addictive than the cigarettes themselves.

PRO TIP

Soak yourself in Febreze to hide your temporary habit.

CIGARETTES 2.0

In 2003, Chinese pharmacist Hon Lik invented the e-cigarette, a device that heats up a nicotine-laced liquid and produces harmless water vapor instead of carcinogenic smoke.

Upgrade to First Class

"Airline travel is hours of boredom interrupted
by moments of stark terror."
—Al Boliska, Canadian radio personality

Once the novelty of featherless flight wears off, the experience of traveling in an airplane is pretty abysmal. Dozens of sweaty, smelly passengers are crammed into miniature seats with nothing but a bag of pretzels and uncomfortable headphones to distract them. Unless, of course, you fly first class.

Sadly first class is expensive, unnecessary, and elitist. But then again, who cares? What's a few extra bucks when your personal comfort is at stake? If it means you can trade in the screaming infants and Salisbury steak for fuzzy slippers and a decent meal, then it's worth it.

You might be able to use some frequent flyer miles to get the first-class bump. If there aren't any trips in your immediate future, then book yourself a short first-class jaunt. You'll feel like a jet-setting movie star, if only for a few hours.

PRO TIP

Book a seat as close to the front as possible. You'll be farther away from the peasants sitting in coach.

TRANSFORM COACH INTO FIRST CLASS

- Mix seltzer and orange juice into makeshift mimosas
- Bring your own bag of macadamia nuts to replace peanuts
- Arrange pillows on your chair for a more comfortable seat

Outsource Your Chores to Neighborhood Children

"My second favorite household chore is ironing. My first being hitting my head on the top bunk bed until I faint."
—Erma Bombeck, humorist

On a 90-degree day, nothing is more unappealing than going outside to do yard work. You'd much rather be lounging inside with a cold glass of lemonade than sweating your butt off for hours on end. Happily the world has been kind enough to provide us with a plethora of people who will gladly do your work, often for minimal payment: children.

Neighborhood kids are perfect for taking care of any and all chores you simply don't want to do yourself, from raking the leaves to repainting the backyard shed. Between the ages of ten and fifteen, kids don't really have any other employment opportunities, so they're usually glad to do anything that will earn them a few bucks for candy, video games, or whatever the hell kids buy these days.

At first you might feel lazy outsourcing your chores to the little tykes. But look at it this way—you're encouraging kids to have a responsible work ethic from a young age, which has to help improve the economy sooner or later.

PRO TIP

Clear everything with the kids' parents before offering them a job—that way people are less inclined to think you're running some sort of weird children's sweatshop in your backyard.

Drink Away Your Sorrows

"I went on a diet, swore off drinking and heavy eating,
and in fourteen days I lost two weeks."
—Joe E. Lewis, comedian

Most of the time, a single glass of wine is enough to take the edge off. Some nights, however, you may require a few dozen to achieve the same effect. Whether it's because you lost your job to someone half your age, or because your car was towed while you were filing divorce papers at the courthouse, there's no shame in drinking your problems away. But if you are going to drown your sorrows in alcohol, you might as well do it right.

Instead of knocking a few back and calling it a night, you're going to drink until you can't feel feelings. And then you're going to drink some more. Find a nice comfy stool at the bar and order up two shots of tequila—one for each hand. Wash it down with a few IPAs and maybe a whiskey sour or two. If the bartender gives you a hard time, tell him to mind his own business and pour you up another.

PRO TIP

Call a cab at the beginning of the night. You might not be able to dial a phone by the end.

DRINKS TO AVOID

- Cement Mixer: Baileys Irish Cream and lime juice (curdles in your mouth)
- Motor Oil: Jägermeister, coconut rum, peppermint schnapps, and cinnamon schnapps
- Nyquil: Sambuca, triple sec, and grenadine

Hit the Snooze Button

*"Blessings on him who invented sleep,
the mantle that covers all human thoughts."*
—Miguel de Cervantes Saavedra, writer

The best moment of your day is when you wake up at 6:00 a.m., look at the clock, and realize you still have another hour and a half to sleep. The worst moment of your day is when what feels like two minutes later, you look at the clock and it reads 7:30 a.m. Your alarm is going off. Time to get up. Or is it?

Do what feels good. Drag that lazy arm out from your side and slam the snooze button. Get your nine additional minutes of sleep. Then when the alarm goes off again, hit the snooze button again. Repeat until you get tired of waking up every nine minutes and just unplug the thing altogether. Collapse effortlessly into your pillows and blankets. It's about time you feel good and refreshed when you wake up. You're not a farmer. Sleep in.

PRO TIP

Keep one eye open to make sure you actually make contact with the snooze button.

Watch a Movie at Work

"The brain is a wonderful organ. It starts working the moment you get up in the morning and does not stop until you get into the office."
—Robert Frost, poet

Rather than fake a sick day—again—go into the office and give off the impression that you're actually hard at work. But instead of polishing off those TPS reports, spend the day catching up on some new releases. Websites like www.hulu.com, www.netflix.com, or even the iTunes store offer a wide selection that is just a mouse click away.

Make some popcorn in the office microwave, and take advantage of that huge computer monitor. Every so often, you'll have to feign some typing or mouse clicking so that your coworkers don't suspect anything. Good headphones are important to pull this off—especially the small earbud ones that are less obvious and can be worn in just one ear.

PRO TIP

Always keep a spreadsheet open, one that's dense with numbers and formulas, so you can quickly click on it and appear to be doing work when your supervisor walks by.

MOVIES ABOUT WORK TO WATCH AT WORK

- *Office Space*, 1999
- *Horrible Bosses*, 2011
- *Nine to Five*, 1980
- *The Promotion*, 2008
- *The Devil Wears Prada*, 2006

Ignore Household Chores

*"My favorite way of getting out of doing chores is
by acting like I'm asleep. But it never works."*
—Devon Werkheiser, actor

It's a beautiful day out, and you've got a sink full of dishes and an
overflowing laundry basket waiting for you. Thus begins the mental battle
of trying to convince yourself that it's better to stay in and clean than to go
outside to frolic.

News flash: it's not. Cleaning sucks, and you should be out enjoying the
fresh air instead of inside inhaling chemical fumes. So today do whatever
the hell you want as long as it doesn't involve cleaning, tidying, vacuuming,
polishing, or scrubbing of any kind.

And don't waste your time feeling guilty about not cleaning. You don't
live in a *Good Housekeeping* photo shoot, and last time we checked, your
name wasn't Monica Geller either. So just get over it and clean tomorrow.

PRO TIP

Leave the house to forget
about the mess.

DO'S AND DON'TS...

- Don't put anything away
- Don't clean the bathtub
- Don't dust the living room
- Do have as many beers as
  you want

Have a Five-Course Meal on Your Lunch Break

"There is no sincerer love than the love of food."
—George Bernard Shaw, Irish playwright

Few things are worse than the sound of an alarm clock pulling you out of a sweet dream and into the cold reality of another workday. When you've hit the snooze button one too many times, there's barely enough time to get dressed and comb your hair, let alone pack a lunch.

Make the best of a bad situation by taking yourself out to lunch—and not just any lunch. Treat yourself to a five-course meal.

You could grab some fast food, but that will never duplicate the complex flavors and nutritional balance of the brown bag lunch you surely would have packed yourself. Only a five-course meal—complete with appetizer, soup, salad, entrée, and dessert—can provide the culinary quality and quantity your body craves. And that's not all. The sophisticated calm of the restaurant offers the perfect atmosphere to rest your mind. At the end of the meal, you'll have gotten all you need for a super-productive afternoon at the office. So what if there are only ninety minutes left in the day? You deserved that three-hour lunch break.

PRO TIP

Don't indulge in a five-course meal if you have a big client meeting or if the boss's boss is in town. You can always pass off your five-course meal as a trial run for an upcoming business dinner, but it will be better if no one notices.

Bump Up Casual Friday to Monday

"Problems are only opportunities in work clothes."
—Henry J. Kaiser, industrialist

Four days each week, you suffer an eight-hour stint in scratchy suits and uncomfortable shoes while Casual Friday glimmers at the end of the workweek tunnel. Unfortunately you can't speed up the calendar—but you can bump up Casual Friday to Monday.

This might seem like laziness or blatant disregard of company policy, but it's nothing of the sort. If anything, it demonstrates how closely you're following the rules.

Just take a look at your job description: it's the same on Mondays as on Fridays, isn't it? Of course it is. So why do you have to be all fancy for the start of the week? Monday isn't any better than Friday. It's not any more important than Friday. And if you've managed to meet company deadlines while decked out in jeans and a T-shirt each Friday, you'll probably be able to do the same on Monday. Even if your productivity does take a dive, your positivity will make a leap in the opposite direction.

PRO TIP

People will take notice of your outfits on Casual Day, and no one wants the office nickname of "Jorts" or "Jersey Shore." Be comfortable, but leave the embarrassing cutoffs and Affliction tees at home.

Go to a Bar Without Money

"Pretty women make us buy beer. Ugly women make us drink beer."
—*Al Bundy,* Married with Children

There are few things more fun than hitting the town with a few friends, placing a credit card on the bar, and ordering up round after round of liquid confidence. Of course this is immediately followed by the miserable task of paying the tab at the end of the night. Luckily tonight you won't be the one left holding the check.

Just this once, leave your wallet at home and rely on your good looks and irresistible charm to score free drinks. Sure, you could afford to buy your own, but you have better things to spend your money on than Jägerbombs.

Belly up to the bar and make yourself look approachable. When a hopeful suitor does buy you a drink, be polite and chat for a while, but not too long. You're here to have fun, not leech off the same person all night. Who knows—along with a few free drinks you might even score a few new friends in the process.

PRO TIP

Always get your drinks directly from the bartender, and never leave a drink unattended.

WHAT YOUR DRINK SAYS ABOUT YOU

- Cosmopolitan: Fun yet sophisticated
- Light beer: Still in college
- Single malt scotch, neat: Tough as nails
- Mojito: High maintenance
- Tequila: You mean business

Dress Up for No Reason

"The more you'll dress up, the more fun you'll have."
—Brian Molko, musician

Hanging in your closet, hidden behind your drab weekly wardrobe, you'll probably find a handful of fancy duds you save only for "special" events. Unfortunately there hasn't been such an event since the turn of the century.

But just because there's nothing special about today doesn't mean you can't create your own excuse to dress up. After all, you spent a lot of money on those fancy clothes, so you might as well get some use out of them for a change.

Get out your most elaborate, expensive outfit, and get ready to show yourself off. Go about your day the same way you would if you weren't dressed to the nines. Activities as simple as going to the grocery store or getting the mail can be "fancy" if you want them to be.

PRO TIP

Avoid places where your expensive clothes won't cause a scene. You want to stand out, after all.

MOST UNDERUSED CLOTHES

- Wedding gowns
- Three-piece suits
- Kilts
- Prom dresses
- Oversized hats

Read a Book on the Phone

"The true art of memory is the art of attention."

—Samuel Johnson, writer

When you hear the phone ring, there's always a moment of panic. Chances are it's that one friend or relative who is just calling to listen to herself talk. Yes, you love your grandma to death, but surely you have better things to do than listen to her drone on about her dry skin for two hours. The good news is that nobody ever said that you actually had to pay attention. Instead of waiting anxiously for the phone to ring, make the call yourself—instant brownie points. Once the gabbing commences, crack the spine of your favorite novel, snuggle into a recliner, and get comfortable. You're going to be here for a while.

PRO TIP

Throw in an occasional "hmm" or "you don't say" to feign interest.

EXCUSES TO END THE CONVERSATION

- "I can't hear you anymore. I think your phone is broken."
- "Is it 7:30 already? Time for bed."
- "Shoot, I forgot I have jury duty. Got to go."

Pimp Your Library Collection

"'Classic.' A book which people praise and don't read."
—Mark Twain, writer

One of the best ways to impress guests is to decorate your home with rows and rows of intelligent, thought-provoking books. Too bad all you actually read are comic books and trashy romance novels. Luckily there is a way to look cool without having to do the work of actual reading. Just buy a bunch of smarty-pants books and fake it.

Go to a used bookstore and pick up all the smart-sounding books you can find. Shakespeare, Dickens, Emily Dickinson, Jane Austen, Poe, Fitzgerald, Freud, Jung, Nietzsche, and Kierkegaard are a good start. The wearier and more broken in they look, the better. It'll look like you actually read them.

Best of all, the chances that anybody will call you out on your ruse are slim. A 2018 poll conducted by the Pew Research Center found that the average person reads only twelve books a year.

PRO TIP

Elevate your bookshelves' front two pegs so your bookcase doesn't fall forward.

THE WORLD'S LARGEST LIBRARY

The Library of Congress is the largest library in the world, with more than 167 million items on approximately 838 miles of bookshelves.

Sneak Dinner Into a Movie

"I'm gonna sneak you into the movies in my tummy!"
—Patton Oswalt, actor and comedian

When a single candy bar or tub of movie theater popcorn costs more than the price of admission, something has gone terribly wrong. Instead of ponying up the cash and grumbling under your breath, it's time you took a stand.

But why stop at a concealed bag of M&M's and a can of soda? Why not go for broke and smuggle in an entire meal? Movies can last upward of three hours these days, and you need your viewing fuel.

Don your baggiest attire (the more pockets, the better), and stuff your person with the contents of your refrigerator: leftover pasta, cheese and crackers, deli meat, and whatever else you have on hand. If you have trouble getting past the ticket taker, just bribe him with a salami.

Now sit back and enjoy the show with all the comforts of your home kitchen. Now you can spend more time enjoying the movie instead of complaining about concession stand price gouging.

PRO TIP

Leave the ice cream at home. A melted puddle of ice cream soup will surely give you away.

EASIEST MEALS TO SNEAK IN

- Burritos
- Sandwiches
- Chicken wings
- Sushi

Take a Three-Hour Lunch Break

"The three-martini lunch is the epitome of American efficiency. Where else can you get an earful, a bellyful, and a snootful at the same time?"
—Gerald R. Ford, US president

With noon rapidly approaching, your brain starts spinning with possible answers to the question that flummoxes workers from Maine to Montana every day: where should I eat lunch? If only you could stretch your hour-long lunch break to an hour and a half... Well, who the hell says you can't? Sure, maybe it's not "encouraged" at your place of business, but then again, neither is *Facebook* stalking, and you don't let that stop you. To keep it semi-legit, just sneak out of the office while your boss is in a meeting—that way, she'll never know how long you've actually been gone.

And while you're at it, turn that hour-and-a-half lunch into two or even three hours. Have multiple courses and a few glasses of wine at the most leisurely restaurant you can think of. Go try on that cute outfit you've been ogling in the Bloomingdale's window for weeks. Or take a stroll in the park to clear your head. Just don't return to work until you've wasted three solid hours of your day. After all, if you're going to do something, you might as well do it right.

PRO TIP

Take along a hat and a large pair of sunglasses to disguise yourself in case you spy the company president at the next table.

Pass Off Takeout as Your Own Cooking

"Please don't lie to me, unless you're absolutely sure I'll never find out the truth."

—Ashleigh Brilliant, writer

Cooking for a crowd can be one of the most stressful activities imaginable. If you don't time everything just right, you're left with burnt food, hungry guests, and a kitchen full of shattered dreams. But even if you aren't a top-rated chef, you can still put together a stellar meal—if you fake it, that is.

Ordering takeout and calling it homemade is certainly misleading, but on the grand scale of dishonesty it barely registers. Your guests get to eat a delicious meal, and you get to pretend you are Julia Child. Everybody wins.

Before your guests arrive, call up your favorite takeout restaurant, pick up a few of its most popular dishes, and stash them in your fridge. Keep everyone out of the kitchen for the entire night (no exceptions), and be sure to bang some pots around and chop up a few loose vegetables for effect. When it's time to serve, reheat the restaurant fare and transfer it into serving dishes. Your guests will never know the difference.

PRO TIP

Quickly dispose of any Styrofoam containers and any other incriminating evidence.

CROWD-PLEASER MEALS

- Bacon-wrapped filet mignon
- Mushroom risotto
- Fettuccine Alfredo
- Maple-glazed pork tenderloin

Become a Meatatarian

*"Vegetables are interesting but lack a sense of purpose
when unaccompanied by a good cut of meat."*
—Fran Lebowitz, writer

These days it seems everyone has some sort of dietary restriction. Some eat only fish, others can't stomach dairy products, and a few won't touch anything that has even been in the same room as a carb.

Well, if you can't beat 'em, join 'em. Today your diet will consist entirely of good old-fashioned animal flesh—like nature intended. While it may not be the healthiest diet ever conceived, it's by far the most delicious. Start yourself off with a few strips of bacon and some breakfast sausage. For lunch try a hamburger or a sandwich without the pesky bun. Finally finish your day off with a thick, bloody steak wrapped in prosciutto with a side of barbecued jumbo shrimp. Resist the urge to supplement your meals with useless vegetables. They're just filler anyway.

PRO TIP

Check labels carefully to ensure no hidden vegetables have contaminated your food.

THE WORLD'S MEATIEST DISH

Dubbed "The Feast," the world's largest meal consists of cooked eggs stuffed into a fish, which is stuffed into chickens, which are stuffed into a sheep, which is stuffed into a camel. The result takes twenty-four hours to cook.

Have a One-Night Stand

"When sex is good there's nothing better, and when it's bad it's not bad."
—Unknown

There's something enticing about the thought of meeting somebody, having a night of wild passion, and then never having to speak to that person again. Unfortunately you aren't that type of person.

Wait a minute—of course you are. Everybody is that type of person! Sure, love and relationships are nice, but every now and then you need to skip all that mushy crap and fast-forward to the fun stuff. And there's nothing wrong with that—as long as your date doesn't extend his or her invitation past one night.

To find your temporary bedmate, belly up to your local bar and scope out the scene. When you spot a potential suitor at your local watering hole, spark up a conversation and keep it casual. Steer the conversation as far away from "relationships" and "intimacy" as possible. You want him or her to think of you purely in the moment. When the timing feels right, invite your pick back to your place for "coffee" (the international code word for sexy time). If he or she agrees, you're good to go. You should be able to take it from here…

PRO TIP

Prepare an exit strategy ahead of time. An early morning meeting or doctor's appointment should get your bedmate out the door.

Leave Your Clean Clothes in the Hamper

"The laundry has its hands on my dirty shirts, sheets, towels, and tablecloths, and who knows what tales they tell."

—Joseph Smith Jr., religious leader

Congratulations! You've tackled the layer of dirty clothes covering the bedroom floor and come out victorious. All you have to do is fold up your now-clean laundry and neatly slide everything into its proper place. If only it were that easy.

After all that sorting, pretreating, loading, drying, and, of course, waiting, you must be exhausted. You can't possibly be expected to deal with hangers and dresser drawers now. Not only do you need a break, you sure as hell deserve one.

Plunk your hamper down on the floor and let it sit while you pour yourself a drink and kick your feet up. If you need any clean clothes, just rifle through and pick out what you need. There's no reason to put everything away just yet. It's certainly not going anywhere.

PRO TIP

Buy a second hamper to use for dirty clothes. Otherwise you will just toss them on the floor and the process will begin anew.

METHODS FOR MINIMIZING LAUNDRY

- Wear only bathing suits
- Line your pockets with air fresheners
- Walk through the car wash on your way home

Blow a Whole Paycheck in One Night

"Whoever said money can't buy happiness simply didn't know where to go shopping."
—Bo Derek, actress

Hallelujah, the most glorious day of days is upon you: payday. Time to be a responsible adult and take care of all those lingering bills and tuck a few extra bucks away for retirement…

Or you could blow your hard-earned cash in a single night. It's not like this is the last paycheck you'll ever receive. You'll have plenty of time to save money later. For now, enjoy yourself. Head to the nearest bank and cash out your entire paycheck in full. Head out on the town and gorge yourself on expensive food, fancy clothes, overpriced drinks, and endless cab rides. Live like royalty for the evening until you collapse from exhaustion or run out of funds—whichever comes first.

PRO TIP

If you don't want to carry around a giant wad of cash, purchase a prepaid debit card for the value of your paycheck.

Take a Mutual Twenty-Four-Hour Break from Your Significant Other

"'Tis better to have loved and lost than never to have loved at all."
—Alfred, Lord Tennyson, poet

As much as you may love your significant other, it can get a little dull doing the same things with the same person day after day. But just because things are getting a little stale doesn't mean your relationship is doomed to failure. Sometimes the best way to spice up your waning love life is to take a little break—if only for twenty-four hours.

Just think: a one-day free pass to do whatever you want with whomever you want with zero consequences. At the end of the day, you can return to your loving, committed relationship as if nothing ever happened.

To begin, be straightforward. Present your no-strings-attached idea as a way to explore your deepest desires without regret. Just remember that boundaries are essential. No twenty-four-hour tryst is worth ruining your relationship over. Unless, of course, said tryst is really, really cute.

PRO TIP

Despite what you may have heard on the playground, the pill does not protect against STDs.

Beat Your Current Sex Record

"If things go well I might be showing her my O-face.
'Oh, oh, oh!' You know what I'm talkin' about."
—*Drew,* Office Space

Sex is like track and field: everyone knows their own personal career record. When you were young and wild, it was standard for you and your significant other to do it twice in the morning right off, once in the afternoon, then three times before bed just to get some shut-eye. Now, with a busier schedule, it's a bit tougher.

Of course, unlike track and field, training for a new sex daily high will require some days off. But that's what'll make the day of the competition that much better. Sit your partner down and explain what you want to accomplish. Not only will you get a day of fun and excitement, but you'll also probably find that your partner is nicer, is more considerate, and listens to you more too.

PRO TIP

Be sure to take some time out of the bedroom to stretch and move around.

MOST DISCONCERTING THINGS TO HEAR DURING SEX

- "Are you sure that's a good idea?"
- "Does it always look like that?"
- "I don't think you're doing it right."
- Any name that isn't your own.

Organize a Game of Strip Poker

"People would be surprised to know how much I learned about prayer from playing poker."
—Mary Hunter Austin, writer

There's that point during every lame party where the six people who actually showed up have to face reality. Nobody else is coming. But don't throw in the towel just yet. There's still a chance to transform your lame gathering into a risqué event that you'll all remember for years to come. All you need is a deck of cards and a bunch of uninhibited party guests.

Wrangle up your small group of partiers and toss your inhibitions to the wind for an impromptu game of strip poker. If your guests were uptight before, you'll be amazed how quickly they loosen up once everyone's half-naked and throwing their underwear onto the table. To make it even more interesting, you can add some wild cards to the game that force players to perform tasks like streaking around the house. It may make a few of your more conservative guests uncomfortable, but at least it's infinitely more exciting than standing in an awkward circle sipping cheap wine.

PRO TIP

Going commando, while sexy, gives you a distinct disadvantage here.

PEOPLE NOT TO INVITE TO STRIP POKER NIGHT

- Family members
- Any morbidly obese people
- Your boss

Scope People Out Unapologetically

"It pays to be obvious, especially if you have a reputation for subtlety."
—Isaac Asimov, writer

When you encounter a particularly smoking hot individual among a sea of ordinary bland faces, you can't help but sneak a tiny peak at the eye candy as it passes you by. But alas, that tiny glimpse is all you get, and it goes by so fast that you've forgotten all the subtle details minutes later.

When you think about it, though, aside from general human decency (which you threw out the window months ago), there's nothing stopping you from feasting your eyes to your heart's content. People that gorgeous require more than a mere glance to fully appreciate, and today you're going to give them the careful consideration they deserve.

Your goal is to be as obvious as possible in your ogling. This means checking people out until it's just as uncomfortable for you as it is for them. Think of it as a staring contest where the rules are reversed. The only way to lose is to actually look the opponent in the eye.

Don't worry about offending anyone. If anything, they should be flattered by your unwavering gaze. It means they've still got what it takes to get some attention—however unwelcome.

PRO TIP

Catcalls of any kind are strongly discouraged. You're creepy, but you aren't a creep. There's a difference.

ESSENTIAL OGLING GEAR

- Mirrored sunglasses
- Wide-brimmed baseball cap
- Cell phone (to pretend to play with)

Hitchhike to the Office

"There's a frood who really knows where his towel is."
—Douglas Adams, writer

Sure, you could drive, bike, or take the bus to work. But all of those methods require some amount of effort or money. It's infinitely easier to just stick out your thumb and hope for the best.

Hitchhiking may be illegal, but it's a great American pastime as old as the car itself. It's also perfectly safe as long as you know what you're doing. To start, position yourself on a busy stretch of road where you're sure to attract attention. Wear something flashy to make yourself more visible, and craft a sign to show potential rides that you're both funny and not crazy— perhaps something like "Come on, do I look like a serial killer?" or "Will give hugs in exchange for rides."

If nobody seems to be biting, resist the urge to show some skin to score a ride, as that will attract only the type of creep you are trying to avoid. Just be patient, and somebody will show up eventually. You may even make a new friend out of the experience.

PRO TIP

Just to be safe, carry some pepper spray to ward off any potential serial killers.

THE HITCHHIKER'S GUIDE TO HITCHHIKING

- Travel alone or with a partner. You'll never get a ride with three or more people.
- Make yourself presentable. Ask yourself: *would I pick me up?*
- Saying please and thank you go a long, long way.

Bake and Eat an Entire Batch of Cookies by Yourself

"In love, as in gluttony, pleasure is a matter of the utmost precision."
—Italo Calvino, writer

Making cookies for friends is a labor of love. You spend hours carefully measuring, sifting, beating, mixing, and baking up tray after tray of delicious cookies, all for the pleasure of watching other people enjoy your creations. If you're lucky, you may get to sample a single cookie before the vultures devour them all.

Well, not this time. Today you're going to be a little selfish and eat every single cookie all by yourself—down to the last crumb. Weight Watchers be damned. There's nothing shameful in consuming twice your weight in baked goods every once in a blue moon. And all that measuring, stirring, and baking burns off a couple of calories anyway. First, don stretch pants—or anything with an elastic waistband—and an apron. Then choose your favorite type of cookie—be it oatmeal raisin, chocolate chip, or gingerbread—set the oven to the necessary temperature, and get measuring.

Eating the batter as you go along, of course, is encouraged. If you start feeling sick, just power through. You aren't a quitter.

PRO TIP

Don't make any plans to leave the house within twelve hours of completing your task.

OTHER FORMIDABLE EATING CHALLENGES

- A whole gallon of milk
- An entire chocolate cake
- A tablespoon of cinnamon

Use the Carpool Lane Alone

*"Americans will put up with anything
provided it doesn't block traffic."*
—Dan Rather, journalist

It's bad enough that you have to sit in traffic, but watching fellow motorists zoom by because they had the foresight to carpool is unbearable. Just this once don't hesitate to sneak into the HOV lane.

You'd like to carpool—it's good for the environment and saves gas—but none of your coworkers live nearby. But just because you can't find a warm body to fill the passenger seat doesn't mean you have to suffer. Rummage around your car for stray clothes, grocery bags, sporting equipment, and anything else you can use to craft a makeshift passenger. It doesn't have to be perfect—just enough to fool a cop at a glance.

Once you've constructed your dummy, slowly merge into the carpool lane and enjoy the rest of your speedy, uneventful commute. Be sure to wave at your fellow solo commuters as you leave them in the dust.

PRO TIP

Adjust your passenger vanity mirror so it obstructs your dummy passenger.

SLUGS INVADE CARPOOL LANES

In some urban areas, a symbiotic relationship known as "slugging" has developed where drivers offer free rides to car-less commuters to utilize carpool lanes.

Chew an Entire Pack of Gum in Ten Minutes

"Well, there are some things you should know. First off, you see gum on the street, you leave it there. It isn't free candy."
—Santa, Elf

It's supersweet, incredibly cheap, and vaguely reminiscent of childhood. Bubble gum is the perfect candy—or it would be if it didn't lose its flavor after twenty-seven seconds.

It's the same sweet song and dance every time. You spring for a pack of watermelon Bubble Yum at the gas station and gleefully unwrap a sticky little block, your mouth watering at the smell. But by the time you've pulled onto the street, the flavor is gone and you're left chomping on a piece of pink rubber.

Say goodbye to that weird sense of loyalty to your bubble gum. Pop a piece in your mouth and enjoy the sweet rush of concentrated flavor. But the second it starts tasting flat, spit it out and unwrap another. At this rate you're going to work through an entire pack in about ten minutes—but at a dollar a pack, you can afford to turn 'em and burn 'em.

PRO TIP

Remember to remove each piece before you pop in another one. Otherwise you risk giving yourself a case of gum-induced TMJ.

THE BEST BUBBLE GUM TO CHEW IN A HURRY

- Bubble Yum
- Dubble Bubble
- Hubba Bubba
- Bubblicious

Stay at an All-You-Can-Eat Buffet All Day

"The US deficit is growing faster than someone
who spent too much time at the all-you-can-eat buffet."
—Andrew Pyle, British philosopher

There is nothing Americans love more than an all-you-can-eat buffet. These little treasures combine two of our favorite things—gluttony and food—into one irresistible package. Unfortunately buffets have one big problem: you can't take any leftovers home.

So next time you hit up an all-you-can-eat venue, make the most of your money by staying the whole damn day. You shelled out $15, and dammit, you're going to eat at least three times that much food. For maximum consumption, you'll want to pace yourself. Start off with something light, like a salad, and then move into the heavier foods like meatloaf and turkey. Finish off with dessert, take a nap, and then repeat the whole process.

To prevent the buffet owner from asking you to leave, you should probably keep a plate of food on your table at all times. But unless the owner can show you a clause on the buffet sign stating that the all-you-can-eat offer is valid for only one meal per day, you're all set for a daylong marathon of gluttony.

PRO TIP

Do not attempt at an Indian buffet unless you want to wreak havoc on your digestive system.

Screw Cancer—Go Out and Bake in the Sun

*"The University of Miami is not a campus
with visible school spirit—just visible tan lines."*
—Lisa Birnbach, journalist

Sun exposure's linkage to skin cancer is perhaps the saddest healthcare revelation of the last few decades. Gone are the days when women would cover themselves with baby oil during marathon outdoor tanning sessions and men would rather endure weeks of sunburn than put on, God forbid, sunscreen.

But even though tanning may be past its prime, don't let the surgeon general prevent you from enjoying the sun. This summer grab your sunscreen (even if it's SPF 4) and scamper outside with your beach towel to soak up as many beautiful golden rays as possible.

Everyone knows people look hotter with tans, and you obviously don't want to be the only pale-faced kid on the block. Plus, sun is a great source of vitamin D—so take *that*, doctor.

PRO TIP

Wear sunglasses to protect
your peepers while tanning.

Crash a Wedding

"Bachelors know more about women than married men;
if they didn't, they'd be married too."
—H.L. Mencken, writer

As long as you aren't involved in the planning portion of a wedding, hanging out at the actual party is a blast. Pity that all of your friends are either already married or forever alone. In order to party it up wedding-style, you're going to have to take matters into your own hands.

On the one hand, crashing a wedding is dishonest, illegal, and potentially dangerous. On the other, it guarantees you unlimited booze, permission to dance like an idiot, and desperate single people as far as the eye can see. Clearly it's worth the risk.

Check newspaper archives for local wedding announcements and start preparing your backstory. When you arrive, head straight for the dance floor and hide among the other drunken partiers. If other guests start asking too many questions, hightail it to the nearest bathroom to throw them off the trail.

Once you've scored a couple of drinks and enjoyed a decent free meal, quietly exit the party—preferably with a bridesmaid or groomsman in tow.

PRO TIP

Use a fake name in case you
encounter a stage-five clinger.

Go Bungee Jumping

"Jump, and you will find out how to unfold your wings as you fall."
—Ray Bradbury, writer

There are few feelings more exhilarating than free fall. Whether it comes from a jump off the high dive or a drop on a roller coaster, once you're free-falling, you have no control over the situation anymore. It's time for you to let go. Experience the ultimate free fall and go bungee jumping. Bungee jumping has been in style ever since Alicia Silverstone did it at the end of the Aerosmith video "Cryin.'" But unlike a jump from an airplane or the fall from a roller coaster, bungee jumping's thrill comes as much from the fall as it does from the rebound. It might be scary, but facing your fears is a big part of life. And it's safe…mostly. Plus, doing some daredevil bungee jumping will give you some much-needed street cred, which you lost that time you jumped behind a bush when a distant firecracker went off.

PRO TIP

Wear a helmet.

THE WORLD'S HIGHEST JUMP

As of 2018, the world's highest commercial bungee jump, according to the Guinness Book of World Records, is at the Macau Tower in China. It stands 764 feet high, more than the length of two football fields.

Run Home for a Nooner

"Women need a reason to have sex. Men just need a place."
—Billy Crystal, comedian

You are trying your best to concentrate on spreadsheets, but for some reason you just can't seem to focus. Perhaps it's because you came into the office to prepare for a 9:00 a.m. meeting instead of fitting in that morning quickie with your significant other.

And now you're stuck waiting until quitting time before you have another chance at sexy time. Or are you?

You came in early this morning, after all. It's not like the office would fall apart if you slipped out for a long lunch—and perhaps a little dessert? Call up your significant other and see if you can arrange for a little lunchtime loving. If home is too inconvenient, now is the perfect time to explore the halfway point between your respective jobs. If you can't find a hotel close by, park in a secluded lot and get busy before anyone realizes what's going on. When you get back to work, the rest of the day should fly by as you revel in your secret little rendezvous.

PRO TIP

Try to keep your clothes off the floor during your noontime getaway. Wrinkles are a dead giveaway.

SECLUDED NOONER LOCALES

- Skeezy hourly hotel
- Restaurant bathroom
- Empty conference room

Have Sex on Your Boss's Desk

"If you think your boss is stupid, remember:
you wouldn't have a job if he was any smarter."
—*John Gotti, mobster*

Perhaps it's part of their DNA, or maybe it's thanks to something in their coffee, but there is one universal fact about every boss in the world—they're all assholes. Each and every one of them. Just once, you're going to stick it to your horrible troll of a boss and pay her back for that time she made you stay late on Friday to organize her collection of antique cookie jars. And what better way to do that than to invite your partner over for a late-night rendezvous and violate your boss's desk?

Wait until the rest of your coworkers are gone, and then check the office and surrounding area for surveillance cameras. Once you are certain it's just you, your partner, and the wall, it's time to scurry into the boss's office and get your revenge on. Make it quick, but make sure you take the time to roll around all over the antique mahogany furniture. Now every time she calls you into her office to chew you out, you can take comfort in the knowledge that your bare butt once rested in the same place she keeps her "Best Boss" coffee mug.

PRO TIP

Resist the urge to chronicle your exploits with a digital camera. The evidence is bound to make its way onto the Internet somehow.

Leave Your Ex's Number on the Bathroom Wall

"There's nothing wrong with revenge—it's the best way to get even!"
—Archie Bunker, All in the Family

Being dumped is about the worst feeling a human being can experience. But once you get over the loss of self-esteem and the unfathomable loneliness, there's only one desire that remains: revenge.

There are a number of ways you can vent your frustration, but unfortunately most of them require a blunt object and a general disregard for personal property. You need an outlet that won't land you in prison. Etching your ex's name and number on a bathroom wall may not seem like much, but it's embarrassing enough to cause damage without resorting to violence. Best of all, it gives you plausible deniability. Hundreds of people have your ex's digits—it could have been anybody.

Grab a marker and hit up every public bathroom within a five-mile radius. Since you are limited in the number you can hit, commission a friend of the opposite gender to ensure full coverage. You may be childish, but you're still thorough. If you start to feel bad, just power through it and keep writing. Your ex always wanted to make new friends. This is just an odd way of making that a reality.

PRO TIP

Disguise your handwriting on the off chance your ex sees it.

Don't Pay Your Bills

"A man who pays his bills on time is soon forgotten."
—Oscar Wilde, writer

It's the first of the month—time to cash your big fat paycheck. Unfortunately it's also time to pay off the stack of bigger, fatter bills accumulating on your counter.

Then again, what's your rush? Those bills have been piling up for weeks. It certainly couldn't hurt to ignore them for a little while longer. It's not like the cable company is going to go under because you didn't pay your $79.95 subscription fee.

Take your overflowing pile of bills and file them under "S" for "some other time." You're still going to pay them—just not today. For now you have more important things to spend your hard-earned money on, like a night on the town or an electric wine chiller—all the things you've always wanted but never had the readily available funds to afford. Don't worry; your bills will still be waiting for you when you get back from your shopping spree.

PRO TIP

Many companies will waive a recent bill if you threaten to cancel the service. It's worth a shot.

METHODS FOR AVOIDING CREDITORS

- Changing your name
- Answering the phone in Spanish
- Declaring bankruptcy
- Good old-fashioned running

Supersize Everything

"Is she fat? Her favorite food is seconds."

—Joan Rivers, comedian

In the good old days the hallmark of a good restaurant was how much food could be crammed onto a single plate. Unfortunately the health-conscious brats of the world have ruined it for everyone.

Despite what some might think, you were not designed to function on a single lettuce leaf and a thimbleful of water. So stop pretending like you can. When you place your lunch order today, keep in mind the following motto: bigger is better.

Upgrade your tiny side of mixed greens to a gargantuan superhero salad complete with hard-boiled eggs, bacon, and heaps of dressing. Forget the tiny chicken sandwich and order a Philly cheesesteak or a footlong meatball sub instead. As for dessert, nothing short of a triple-scoop sundae with hot fudge, chopped nuts, and a mountain of whipped cream will suffice.

You'll know you've had enough when your pants button pops off or the restaurant asks you to leave—whichever comes first.

PRO TIP

Never attempt this act of extreme gluttony on a first, second, or even twenty-seventh date. In fact, you probably should go this one solo.

"DO YOU WANT TO DINO-SIZE THAT?"

McDonald's originally released its "Supersize" fries and sodas in 1993 as "Dino-Sized" to capitalize on the popular movie *Jurassic Park*. The company changed the name after the promotion.

Order a Kids' Meal

"Never eat more than you can lift."

—*Miss Piggy,* The Muppets

There's no denying it—fast food makes you fat. Unfortunately it also happens to be delicious. Fortunately there is a way to enjoy its wonderful, greasy goodness without all the guilt. Instead of ordering a milkshake, large fries, and a triple-decker bacon cheeseburger, turn your attention to the kids' menu. Sure, you're decades past adolescence, but deep down you're still a kid.

So pick your favorite fast-food option and order it up in kids' meal form. The portions are smaller, the taste is the same, and you get a fun toy to play with too. Bonus points if you play in the indoor playground when you're done.

PRO TIP

Do not put the toy in your mouth. It's a choking hazard.

UNHEALTHIEST KIDS' MEALS

- McDonald's Mighty Kids Meal: Double cheeseburger, fries, chocolate milk

- Wendy's Kids' Meal: Chicken nuggets, fries, chocolate Frosty

- KFC Kids' Meal: Popcorn chicken, potato wedges, string cheese, soda

Don't Bring Anything to a Potluck

"Have something to bring to the table,
because that will make you more welcome."
—Randy Pausch, educator

With the advent of the dreaded potluck, the onus of the meal was lifted off the host and placed like a yoke onto the shoulders of the event's poor guests. While you probably want to spend time with your friends, you probably don't want to spend a whole bunch of time making a huge dish that you have to transport hot to someone else's home. In this case it's not like you even get to keep the leftovers! It's time to shrug off the yoke and show up empty-handed.

The next time you find yourself invited to a potluck, simply show up at the door with nothing but a broad smile and a big appetite. There are plenty of excuses to use for your lack of contribution, but you shouldn't have to explain yourself. You didn't bring anything because you're the guest—plain and simple.

PRO TIP

Be prepared for a lot of no-shows the next time you throw a dinner party.

REASONS POTLUCKS SUCK

- You never get back your Tupperware.
- It's hard to transport food without ruining it.
- One casserole is delicious. Ten are disgusting.

Abuse the Student Discount

"Living in the past has one thing in its favor—it's cheaper."
—Unknown

Students sure do have the life. They can sleep until noon, eat pizza for every meal, drink like a fish—and get discounts using their student IDs. Time may have taken its toll, but you still slightly resemble the picture on your old student ID. Why not use it to get the same perks you did as an undergrad? Passing as an undergrad will not only help you save a few bucks to put toward your college loans, but it'll also convince people that you're younger than you are.

Next time you're at a movie or museum, whip out the college ID and put on your best "I survive solely on ramen noodles" face. Chances are the person ringing you up won't give it a second thought. You spent thousands to go to college—why not stretch it a little further?

PRO TIP

Don't lose your ID. Once you're years removed from the school, it's virtually impossible to order a new one.

BEST PLACES TO USE A STUDENT ID

- Movies
- Museums
- Amusement parks
- Bars and nightclubs
- Restaurants

Steal a Magazine from the Doctor's Office

"The more that you read, the more things you will know.
The more that you learn, the more places you'll go."
—Dr. Seuss, writer

For years you've endured pokes, prods, and pricks at the hands of your cruel GP. But the worst part about going to the doctor's office is not being able to finish that article you were reading when you were called into the exam room. Today is the day you strike back against the unfairness of a place that both makes you sit in a cold room in a paper robe and doesn't allow you to find out what exactly happened on the season finale of *Keeping Up with the Kardashians*. Perhaps it's time you swiped a little something extra for your trouble.

On your way out of the office, nonchalantly wander past the magazine shelf and pick up the magazine you were reading before the nurse so rudely interrupted you. Before anyone notices, just roll it up, tuck it under your arm, and head for the exit. Now you can finish that article whenever you want—without worrying about impending needles.

> **PRO TIP**
> ....
> Be prepared to find a new
> doctor if anybody catches on.

Play in the Mud

"There is an eagle in me that wants to soar, and there is a hippopotamus in me that wants to wallow in the mud."
—Carl Sandburg, writer and poet

You're an upstanding adult, so one expectation after another is piled on your shoulders. Make sure your hands are clean. Keep your clothes neat. Look respectable. Cinderelly, Cinderelly, Cinderelly!

But sometimes isn't it fun to do the opposite of what's expected? Now we're not suggesting that you stop showering or start pulling on dirty clothes from the hamper. You're just taking a break from cleanliness. The best way—by which we mean the most fun way—is to play in the mud. If you ever played an outdoor sport, you know what we're talking about. The rain games are the best games.

If you're feeling nostalgic, reconnect with your inner child over a stack of mud pies. If you're looking for a facial on the cheap, slather the stuff across your face and arms. Artistic types can etch their artwork into the mud canvas. Feeling rambunctious? Call up some friends, and set up a mudball fight and a natural slip and slide. And once your friends are there and in on the fun, the possibilities are endless.

Come on—you can send out your laundry tomorrow.

PRO TIP

If you're wary of hosing down your own backyard, wait for a summer rainstorm and head to the nearest park. Bring a soccer ball in case anyone asks how you managed to tear up a whole field.

Feed Your Pets Filet Mignon

"We can judge the heart of a man by his treatment of animals."
—Immanuel Kant, German philosopher

Pets are the perfect companion. They never judge when your dignity's gone out the window, and they're always up for a good snuggle. The only thing they ask for in return is food. Whether your cat smells a tuna fish sandwich or your dog spots a fallen crumb, it goes nuts over anything edible.

Yet perversely a pet's one joy is met with nothing more than dry pet food pebbles. Shouldn't you give your pet something to really purr over? In people terms, the crème de la crème of dining is filet mignon. Bring the French cuisine to the pet bowl and let your pet enjoy meat the way it should be. Shut off any thoughts about price or dietary concerns, and simply witness the pure delight as your furry companion chows down. You can even turn it into a dinner for two and pull up a chair and your own filet. After this meal there will be no doubt that your pet will love you for life.

PRO TIP

A whole filet is a choking hazard, not to mention a mess. Be sure to cut the filet mignon into bite-sized pieces.

LAP OF LUXURY

- Couch time on the "forbidden" love seat
- One-hour petting session
- Visit to the aquarium (cat)
- Visit to the tennis court (dog)

Cancel All Your Meetings

"A meeting moves at the speed of the slowest mind in the room."
—Dale Dauten, business consultant

Just when you thought you were actually going to get some work done, your diligent computer calendar sends you a foreboding alert. Drop everything—it's meeting time.

Of all the copious distractions and time sucks in an office, nothing destroys productivity better than a group of people talking in circles for an hour. So why do you bother going?

Think about all of the times something useful has come out of a meeting you attended. Can you count them on one hand? One finger? Open up your calendar and wipe your day clean of every brainstorming session, progress report, team check-in, and anything that even resembles a meeting. Pretend to fall ill, invent an off-site project, whatever it takes. Just don't go within 100 feet of a conference room. Instead of just sitting around talking about doing things, today you are actually going to get things done. It should be a novel experience.

PRO TIP

Take your computer away from your desk to work so nobody can track you down and drag you to a meeting.

THINGS WORSE THAN MEETINGS

- Performance reviews
- Company socials
- Organized company softball

Buy a Round for the Bar (On Someone Else)

"I feel sorry for people who don't drink. When they wake up in the morning, that's as good as they're going to feel all day."
—Frank Sinatra, musician

After you've kicked back a few, it's only natural to want to share your newfound euphoria with the rest of the bar in the form of a round of drinks. Sadly the contents of your wallet—two singles and a coupon for free coffee—just aren't going to cut it. Desperate times call for desperate measures, and if you want to be the hero of the bar, you'll have to outsource the financial responsibility.

Walk up to the bar and proudly order a round of drinks for everyone. Inform the bartender that the creepy guy in the corner offered to pick up the tab (let's call him Sea Bass). Give old Sea Bass a reassuring wave, and when he responds in kind, he will have unwittingly agreed to pay for everyone's booze.

Sure, it's juvenile and dishonest, but it's not like Sea Bass is actually going to be held accountable. He'll sort everything out with the bartender later, but not before everyone has already consumed the evidence and you're miles out of reach of any potential backlash.

PRO TIP

Don't pull this stunt at a bar you would like to revisit in the future.

Organize a Beer Olympics

"The Olympics remain the most compelling search for excellence that exists in sport, and maybe in life itself."
—Dawn Fraser, Australian athlete

Like blue jeans, alcohol goes well with everything. Whether you're on a first date or watching the president's State of the Union address, drinking has a special place in our most enjoyable activities.

One area where we could use more alcohol, though, is in our competitive sports. That's why you'd be doing yourself and society a favor by organizing a beer Olympics. Beer Olympics can include softball, a three-legged race, and that game where you spin your head on the heel of a baseball bat five times and then try to cross the finish line. Incorporate alcohol into all of that. Not only will it be fun, it'll be educational: you'll see which of your friends has a real tolerance. You can even have a medal ceremony. It's not really drinking; think of it instead as a more challenging way to exercise.

PRO TIP

Have a designated puking station, especially for Beer Dizzy Bat.

THE SIMPLEST BEER OLYMPICS GAME

Pick a word at the beginning of the night. Every time someone says that word: DRINK!

Stage a Food Fight

"Food should be enjoyed rather than endured."
—Steve Hamilton, writer

As you sit down to another boring egg salad sandwich, you realize lunchtime as an adult is exponentially less fun than it was when you were a kid. There's no cool-kids table, hardly anyone trades snacks, and there's nary a PB&J sandwich in sight.

To liven things up, it's going to take more than a few stray armpit farts. What this situation calls for is a good old-fashioned food fight. Without warning, duck behind the nearest chair and hurl pieces of your sandwich at unsuspecting coworkers. Chances are they will be too shocked to retaliate at first, which will give you a tactical advantage in the battle. As others join in, duck and weave your way around the office, launching food bombs as you go. When everyone runs out of food, dust yourselves off and return to your desks as if nothing happened. Sound silly? Perhaps. But you'll be amazed at how easily a few macaroni-and-cheese bombs can improve office morale and solidify you as the office "cool kid."

PRO TIP

Don't wear your best suit on food fight day. It's just common sense.

BEST FOODS FOR A FOOD FIGHT

• Mashed potatoes
• Macaroni and cheese
• Chili
• Tuna casserole
• Anything with peas

Make Your Significant Other Sleep on the Couch

"When I'm alone, I can sleep crossways in bed without an argument."
—Zsa Zsa Gabor, actress

Sharing the bed with someone has many upsides—rampant cuddling, spontaneous morning sex, consistent spooning. But everything has its downsides, and speaking of downsides, why won't your boyfriend/girlfriend move over and quit hogging the goddamn covers all the time?

Yes, there are some things even a king-sized bed can't fix. It's okay to want to stretch out once in a while. So tonight tell your loved one, "Sorry, honey, you're sleeping on the couch." After all, it's only one night. Think of the possibilities! You could sleep right in the center of the bed. You could sleep diagonally with your head in one corner and your feet in the opposite. You could stretch out horizontally. You could wrap yourself up in the comforter like a human hot dog.

And how sweet it is. Once you've had your fill of sleeping solo, you'll be happy to invite a warm body back into the bed. But if you're going to brag about it, be prepared to be exiled occasionally yourself.

PRO TIP

Couches are optional—if you have a guest bed, that'll do too.

Cut in Line

"If they gave me four dollars, I'd wait in line."
—David Williams, comedian

You are an important person with important things to do. You can't waste your time standing around. So don't! If the only thing standing between you and the counter is a line of your peers, feel free to jump in.

Make sure that you're mentally ready to dodge the queue. When you arrive at the line, stand next to the person who's waiting in front of you rather than behind him or her. Check out any magazines or candy bars in the aisle so you appear distracted. Edge up to the counter and quickly move to the front. Do not look back.

Remember that you've been jumped in line plenty of times. Think of this small act of defiance as evening out the cosmic balance.

PRO TIP

Watch out for flying objects thrown by the pissed-off people behind you.

PEOPLE TO AVOID PISSING OFF

- Pregnant women
- The elderly
- Anyone with multiple body piercings

Sneak Into Your Neighbor's Pool

"I've just been handed an urgent and horrifying news story.
I need all of you to stop what you're doing and listen. Cannonball!"
—Ron Burgundy, Anchorman

In summertime nothing beats a day at the pool. You stretch out as a warm breeze filters across your sun-kissed skin, allowing your body to find true relaxation. Then right on cue, hordes of screaming children run toward the waterslide, and the afternoon rush of gabbing soccer moms arrive to ruin your peaceful day.

You are in desperate need of something a little more private. Luckily you have a neighbor. Your neighbor has a pool. So by the transient nature of property, you also have a pool.

Today you're going to pull on your swimsuit and take control of that pool as though you're the one paying the pool boy to clean it. You can even bring along some snacks and a pitcher of margaritas for the party. After all, what your neighbors don't know won't hurt them. To avoid arousing suspicion, you should probably wait until nightfall—or at least until midday when your neighbors have all gone to work—to stake your claim. It's less likely that you'll be seen that way. Even better, wait until your neighbors have gone on vacation.

PRO TIP

To avoid a potential 911 call, limit your
pool party to four people or fewer.

"Borrow" a Coworker's Lunch

"What's mine is mine, and what's yours is mine too."
—Unknown

If your office is like the rest of corporate America, the break room has plenty of coffee to boost your energy and an endless supply of oversized water jugs. But if you want real food, you're out of luck. Fortunately for you there's a free supply of real food hidden away—you just have to walk into the communal kitchen and crack open the refrigerator door.

Sure, the scattered homemade lunches aren't technically open for public consumption, but your coworkers really can't expect a brown paper bag to deter someone as hungry—and as selfish—as you are. Besides, based on the garbage they're bringing to work every day, you're doing them a favor by forcing them to splurge on takeout.

So while everybody is plugging away at their spreadsheets and progress reports, sneak away from your desk and swipe an unattended brown bag from the kitchen. Since you are dealing with stolen goods, just scarf down the contents right there and dispose of any incriminating evidence. Finders keepers, losers weepers.

PRO TIP

Check yourself for stray crumbs before you return to your desk. The devil is in the details.

Embellish Your Resume

"I hand him the single greatest work of fiction
known to man: my resume."
—Tyler Knight, writer

Finding a job remains as difficult as ever. Some jobs receive thousands of applicants, all more qualified than the next. How are you supposed to compete with resume points like Harvard, MBA, and Special Olympics volunteer?

Easy: embellish your resume. In case your prospective employer does a background check, it's probably not smart to lie about your GPA or current job title. But it's safe and easy to exaggerate your current and past job responsibilities. "Assisted with networking reception logistics" becomes "Coordinated and managed networking reception logistics," and so on. Just be careful not to fib too much—otherwise it could bite you in the ass if your new employer demands your "expertise" on something you know nothing about. If at first you feel nervous embellishing your resume, don't be. How do you think everyone else out there is getting jobs?

PRO TIP

Don't lie about things that can be easily verified, such as your criminal history or your college major.

RISKY RESUMES

A 2017 survey from HireRight found that 85 percent of employers found applicants lying on their resumes.

Cool Off in a Public Fountain

"The cistern contains: the fountain overflows."
—William Blake, poet and artist

It's the middle of the day, it's oppressively hot and humid, and there's no relief in sight—unless, of course, you want to dive headfirst into a public fountain.

Come to think of it, that's exactly what you want to do. You're hot, and there's a nice cool supply of water right there. It's a no-brainer really. When it comes to swimming in what is essentially a sculpture, approach doesn't really matter. Feel free to slowly wade in or kick off your sandals and do a cannonball right into the center. Regardless of how you go about it, you're sure to attract some dirty looks. Don't pay them any attention, though. You're as cool as a cucumber now, and that's all that matters.

PRO TIP

Bring a change of clothes to work unless you're comfortable sitting around in your underwear.

ROME'S LARGEST FOUNTAIN

Standing over 85 feet high and almost 161 feet wide, the Trevi Fountain is the largest fountain in Rome and is perhaps the world's most famous fountain.

Park Wherever You Want

"Politics ain't worrying this country one-tenth
as much as where to find a parking space."
—Will Rogers, humorist

For some reason the world's city planners have decreed that all the best places to park would instead be used for fire hydrants, loading zones, bus stops, and taxi stands. Not exactly convenient when you are late for a lunch meeting.

A better person would drive around aimlessly and hope for the best, but not you. You gave up being a sap months ago. Today you're going to park wherever you want, and the cops and meter maids can just deal with it.

Stop praying to the parking space gods, and make a beeline for the nearest empty section of curb. Even if there are dozens of signs that say "Don't Even Think about Thinking about Parking Here," just pull right up, lock the car, and go about your business. You can worry about the inevitable parking ticket later. For now, just enjoy your lunch.

PRO TIP

Handicapped spaces are still off-limits. You're selfish, not heartless.

MOST POPULAR PARKING METHODS

• Camping: Pull over and monitor a single street
• Stalking: Follow people to their cars
• Wedging: Squeeze into a space that's too small and climb out the window

Get the House to Yourself

"I don't want to be alone. I want to be left alone."
—Audrey Hepburn, actress

Family togetherness is a wonderful thing. Not half as wonderful, however, as having the entire house to yourself.

It's not that you don't love your family; it's just that sometimes everybody wants a little alone time, which can be very difficult to obtain with a spouse, three kids, two dogs, and a fish.

Brainstorm a series of fool's errands that will keep your family occupied for a few hours. Draft an excessive shopping list, or break a few essential household items and send everyone out for replacements—anything to get them out of the house and out of your hair. With the house to yourself, you are free to do whatever you want. Eat all the junk food you want, invite your friends over for an impromptu poker game, or just sprawl out on the couch with a book. Just make sure not to do any irreparable damage, or you may never get the house to yourself again.

PRO TIP

Some people are more efficient than others. Give your family twice as many errands as you believe necessary, just to be safe.

Charge a Personal Item to the Company

"I haven't reported my missing credit card to the police because whoever stole it is spending less than my wife."
—Ilie Nastase, Romanian tennis player

In the age of corporate credit cards, it can be incredibly tempting to charge something for yourself to the company. After all, most companies are highly profitable, and yet they continue paying you barely enough to live on. So next time the urge to buy strikes, go for it.

It wouldn't be prudent to charge an obvious large-ticket item like a new bike to your company. Instead, charge something small from an inconspicuous vendor—like a new planner from FedEx Office or a book from your local bookstore. If you lump your goody in with other items that you actually need for work, the chances of anyone noticing your rogue purchase are minimal. And if you're really nervous about this undertaking, buy something supercheap, like a candy bar or a soda. You'll still have the opportunity to feel like a badass.

PRO TIP	FOR A HAMBURGER TODAY...
Don't make a habit of charging personal items to the company, unless you want to land in jail.	The modern credit card was first used in the 1920s to sell fuel to automobile owners.

Order One of Everything

"You get fat in the moments between when you know you should stop and when you do."

—Michael Lipsey, artist

Everyone knows the most difficult part of dining out is not picking a neighborhood or even a restaurant in which to eat, but something much more critical—selecting your meal. Do you want fish or steak? Pasta or salad? Sometimes the choices are so voluminous that there is only one logical decision: order one of everything.

Your wallet is obviously going to take a hit from an activity such as this, but obvious benefits exist as well. You'll minimize ordering time and maximize eating time. You'll know exactly what you do and don't like on the menu. And you'll obviously have a fridge packed with leftovers once you're able to waddle home.

So go ahead and order it all—from the crab cakes to the chocolate cake. Gluttony is a word usually reserved for food-based festivities and cookouts, but let's be honest—shoveling huge amounts of food into your face twice a year just isn't enough.

PRO TIP

Wear stretch pants. Otherwise your jeans are likely to burst open midmeal.

OFFSET THE MEAL COST BY...

- Coercing a friend into dining with you
- Slipping a dead bug into your ravioli
- Dining and dashing

Shave Your Head

"I'm undaunted in my quest to amuse myself by constantly changing my hair."

—Hillary Clinton, politician

Long, luscious, wavy hair is considered sexy in most of the world. Unfortunately it also happens to be a royal pain in the ass to maintain. And for those not blessed with gorgeous locks, there's the never-ending battle with cowlicks, widow's peaks, and split ends. It's enough to make you wonder if you wouldn't be better off without it.

Just imagine it for a moment: no more curlers, no more straightening irons, no more hair gel, no more scrambling with a towel when you get out of the shower. Just a smooth, sensual, bald head. It's what you've always wanted but never had the nerve to do.

Trim your locks down with scissors first, and then grab a fresh razor and head to the bathroom. Take one last look at that frustrating widow's peak and kiss your rat's nest goodbye. Once you are fully shorn, head out for a drive and revel in the warm air whipping around your shiny new chrome dome. You'll be the envy of everyone you see. And if not, it's just hair. It'll grow back—eventually.

PRO TIP

Invest in a decent hat in case you aren't pleased with the results.

Haze the New Guy at Work

"We really did have a club whose members jumped from the branch of a very high tree into the river as initiation."

—John Knowles, writer

Let's face it: nobody likes the new guy at the office. He's smug, standoffish, and far too full of himself for somebody who's been there only a week. Perhaps it's time to knock him down a few pegs with some good old-fashioned hazing.

Since fraternity-style hazing is a little too intense for the office—and a little too illegal—settle for smaller pranks like encasing the newbie's stapler in Jell-O or gluing his mouse to his desk. Explain how much the boss likes it when his employees call him T-Bone or how Wednesday is "dress like your favorite superhero" day.

You can even enlist the rest of your office and come in early to cover his cubicle with sticky notes. Think of it as a team-building exercise that will bring everyone closer together—everyone except for the new guy, that is.

PRO TIP

It's best to do most hazing while your boss is out of the office.

RULES FOR HAZING

- If he starts crying, you've gone too far
- Don't damage anything irreparably
- If you're caught, deny, deny, deny

Sneak Into a Hotel Pool

"Free is the best. Anything free is good."
—Sandra Bullock, actress

Swimming pools offer some of life's greatest summertime pleasures: hot sun, comfy lounge chairs, and refreshing water. But unless you fork out for a country club membership or hang out with the teenyboppers at the super-chlorinated community center pool, they're off-limits to you.

That is, unless you pretend to be a guest at the nearest hotel. These days every decent hotel has a pool. The good ones even have a hot tub and baskets of fluffy terry cloth towels. With a constant stream of guests in and out of the hotel lobby, it's impossible for the concierges to keep track of who belongs and who doesn't.

Remember to act like you belong. Skip the front desk and walk straight to the elevators, where you'll be sure to find a gold plaque directing you to the swimming pool. Once you're there, unwind by soaking up some rays and perfecting your swan dive. While you're congratulating yourself on having gotten the best of the country club with none of the membership fees, remember to slip out a side exit.

PRO TIP

You don't want to look like you're coming to the hotel just to go swimming, so leave the pool noodles and inner tube at home.

Invent a Vacation

"The real voyage of discovery consists not in seeking new landscapes but in having new eyes."
—Marcel Proust, writer

Tired of seeing everybody gloat about their exotic travels while you can hardly pay the rent each month? Don't get mad—get even.

Today you're going to give those smug bastards a taste of their own medicine and invent the vacation of a lifetime. First, choose your dream destination. The sky's the limit here since you won't actually be leaving your chair. A quick *Google* search and some Photoshop magic later, and you've suddenly got an entire slideshow's worth of memories.

Fake pictures in hand, create an online album with an obnoxious title—*Jet-Setting to Paris!!!*—and send it to all of your smug, travel-happy friends. With any luck they'll be so busy planning their counter trip that they won't notice you're wearing the same clothes in every picture.

PRO TIP

Make sure your trip is humanly possible. You can't have a photo in London at noon and another in Sydney three hours later.

BEST VACATIONS TO INVENT

- Backpacking in Nepal
- African safari
- Sailing in the Greek Islands
- Bike tour of France

Get a Tattoo

"I am a canvas of my experiences, my story is etched in lines and shading, and you can read it on my arms, my legs, my shoulders, and my stomach."

—Kat Von D, tattoo artist

Some people change their appearance by the hour, but most of us pretty much look the same whether it's Monday, Saturday, March, or November. There's a lot to be said for consistency, but sometimes you've got to shake things up a little.

And what better to break you out of your cookie-cutter monotony than a spontaneous tattoo? Sure, you are glad that you never got that butterfly on your ankle when you were a teenager, but you're all grown up now and better qualified to handle such a permanent life decision.

The wonder of tattoos is that there is no right or wrong. If you've always wanted Yosemite Sam blazed across your chest, then by all means, get it done. Think a golden Triforce on your hand is too nerdy? Think again. You are limited only by your imagination—and your boldness.

PRO TIP

Draw the tattoo in marker first before you make it a permanent part of your body.

WHAT YOUR TATTOO SAYS ABOUT YOU

- Bicep: Hyperaggressive
- Lower back: Skanky
- Hand: Overconfident
- Face: Psychopathic
- Top of the foot: Insecure

Stage a Subway Dance Party

"There is a bit of insanity in dancing that does everybody a great deal of good."
—Edwin Denby, poet

Anyone who has ever ridden the subway knows there is one golden rule of commuting: you do not, under any circumstances, attempt to engage your fellow commuters. No eye contact, no smiling, and absolutely no talking.

Today, armed with a boom box and a total disregard for public humiliation, you are going to give your fellow subway drones a break from the constant monotony. They may not realize it, but deep down they are dying for a good old-fashioned dance party. If nothing else, it will give them something to talk about when they reach their destination.

While a boom box or a cell phone with a speaker are ideal, you can simply belt out your favorite tune and bust out your least embarrassing dance moves to start your impromptu episode of *Soul Train*. If the other passengers don't join in right away, don't be discouraged—your contagious enthusiasm will soon win them over.

PRO TIP

Plan your dance party around busy commuting times. There isn't enough room to turn around during rush hour, let alone dance.

Go on a "Supermarket Sweep" at the Grocery Store

"They don't have a decent piece of fruit at the supermarket. The apples are mealy, the oranges are dry. I don't know what's going on with the papayas!"

—*Kramer,* Seinfeld

There's no need to concern yourself with such delicate and time-consuming aisles like the produce department or the deli counter when doing a "supermarket sweep." No. The point here is to race through the grocery store as fast as possible while filling your shopping cart as much as possible. Have a friend time you, putting two minutes on the stopwatch and counting down across the PA system when you have only ten seconds to go.

On the show *Supermarket Sweep*, the best part was always the cereal aisle. The contestants would fly past the shelves, scooping row upon row of boxes into their carts as they went. Follow suit by stocking up on packaged desserts, pasta sauce, olives—whatever you pass by belongs in the cart. Canned corn? You'll take twenty. Pickles? You'll need at least fifteen. It's not like you have a shopping list, so there's really nothing to forget. Chances are you'll never actually be on a game show, so now's the time to indulge your fantasy.

PRO TIP

Since money is no object here, make sure you have enough in your account to cover your purchases. Also helpful is a car big enough to get all those boxes of cereal home.

Jet-Set for the Afternoon

"If some people didn't tell you, you'd never know they'd been away on a vacation."

—Kin Hubbard, humorist

One of the best ways to pass the time during a slow work afternoon is to think of all the exotic places you'd rather be. If only you were a rich socialite instead of an underpaid desk jockey.

Then again, while you may not have mountains of cash to travel the world, you can certainly scrape together enough for a short twenty-four-hour jaunt. You may have to dip into your rainy day fund, but isn't that precisely what it's there for?

Forget itineraries or researching ticket prices online; just throw a few essentials into a bag and head straight for the airport. Pick a destination at random (Paris, Tahiti, Buenos Aires, London), and hop on the first available flight. Don't worry about minor details like where you'll stay or what you'll do once you arrive; you have the whole flight to figure that out.

PRO TIP

Stick with just a carry-on bag. If you need to check a bag, you don't understand the concept of jet-setting.

JET-SETTING ESSENTIALS

- Oversized sunglasses
- Small dog(s)
- Limo driver
- American Express Black Card

Drink an Entire Bottle of Wine by Yourself

"I cook with wine. Sometimes I even add it to the food."
—W.C. Fields, actor

It's been a long day, and your frustrations just seem to keep multiplying. After work you walk in the door, throw down your keys, and immediately head for the wine rack. You pour a glass or two, willing away your workplace woes. You know it would be smart to put the bottle away, but tonight you really just don't want to.

So don't. Instead, kick off your shoes, order delivery, and treat yourself to not one or two glasses of wine, but the whole darn bottle. Everybody needs a little extra vino in their system now and then, and drinking a whole bottle in one night merely means you're a fun-loving soul—not that you're an alcoholic.

Whether you crack open a bottle of the cheap stuff or dig into a bottle of vintage Cab that's been sitting in your wine rack for months, feel free to drink away. After all, studies have shown both red and white wines to be heart-healthy, and who doesn't want a working ticker?

PRO TIP

Drink several glasses of water before bed to reduce the risk of hangover.

Bet It All on Black

"You cannot beat a roulette table unless you steal money from it."
—Albert Einstein, scientist

To be a successful gambler, you could study probabilities and spend countless hours grinding out wins and losses to come out ahead. Or you could always bypass all that and just go for broke.

Betting your hard-earned cash on a spinning wheel may seem stupid, but how is it any different from playing the stock market? Besides, it's your money, and you are well within your rights to fritter it away however you choose.

Head to the casino and walk straight to the roulette wheel. Whether you want to bet $10 or $10,000, your next move is the same: convert it to chips and smack it down right on black. If you win, cash out your earnings and spend it on anything from an expensive meal to a new car. Just don't stick around the casino to find out how quickly you can lose it.

PRO TIP

Leave your credit cards and extra cash at home to remove temptation should you lose.

ROULETTE ODDS

• Any single number: 37:1
• Row 00 (00 or 0): 19:1
• First column: 2.167:1
• Black/red: 1.111:1

Drive at Your Own Speed

"You're only here for a short visit. Don't hurry, don't worry.
And be sure to smell the flowers along the way."
—Walter Hagen, professional golfer

Whether you're touring a national park or admiring that lovely field of poppies on the way home from work, go ahead and slow down—and don't apologize for it either.

Why? Because in a world that moves faster than the speed of light, sometimes the only moment of Zen you can hope for is a glimpse of grazing deer along the road or a stunning sunset on a Tuesday night commute. Besides, according to the EPA, you may conserve as much as 25 percent more gas while you slow down to enjoy the view—which is good for the environment and your wallet.

So slow down, take it in, and don't worry about the number on the street sign or the honking horns. Don't waste your time feeling bad for anyone behind you either. Turns out there's a simple solution—it's called "going around."

PRO TIP

Flash any irritated drivers a big smile and a wave as they pass. Save the finger for when they're out of eyeshot.

Ignore Your Email

"I often work by avoidance."
—Brian Eno, musician

Think of all the time you spend on your work computer, constantly being distracted by that small ping signifying yet another pointless email. You don't need to look at yet another forward from the coworker you avoid in the lunchroom, and you don't need yet another update on your office's wellness goals from HR. In fact, if it weren't for email, think of all the work you'd get done. Alas, office etiquette forces you to reply, forward, and carbon-copy all day long. But sometimes you need a vacation from your inbox too.

Don't bother setting up an automated response. Just close out your inbox and leave it closed. Without having to respond to inane emails, you'll have the entire day to catch up on your expense reports and maybe even brainstorm a new project idea. You'll be amazed at what you can accomplish when you aren't pulled away every five minutes.

Your coworkers may be a little peeved that you're ignoring them, but the unexplained shunning may just force them to fix their own problems for a change.

PRO TIP

Avoid the wrath of your boss by setting up shop in a vacant conference room. Just make sure no big meetings are scheduled there that day.

OUT-OF-THE-OFFICE AUTO-RESPONSE IDEAS

- Day trip to visit your grandmother
- Pet emergency at the vet
- Volunteering at the local shelter
- Twenty-four-hour flu

Order the Most Expensive Menu Item on a First Date

"You should order the most expensive thing on the menu,
so he knows you're worth it."
—Phyllis Vance, The Office

The candles are glowing, the wineglasses are brimming, and the conversation is punctuated by awkward pauses that can mean only one thing: a terrible first date.

Normally you would stick to a reasonably priced yet mildly dull entrée like roasted chicken or lasagna. But since your date is as dull as an old knife, you might as well venture into more expensive territory. Whether you've got a craving for crab legs or a passion for prime rib, go ahead and order up. If the date takes a turn for the better, your companion will know you're a sophisticated gourmet who enjoys the finer things in life. And if things continue to go less than swimmingly, at least a delicious $50 entrée will give you something to tell your friends about.

So sit back, relax, and enjoy another bite of filet mignon. You can always get lasagna next time—when it's your turn to pay.

PRO TIP

Pretend to be at least moderately interested in your date. Otherwise you might find yourself paying for the coq au vin.

Don't Bother Washing Your Hands

"You know when I wash my hands? When I shit on them!
That's the only time! And you know how often that happens?
Tops, tops, two, three times a week, tops."

—George Carlin, comedian

Our modern society is obsessed with cleanliness. We shower twice a day, we carry little sanitizer bottles with us at all times, and we'd rather die than eat something that fell on the floor. Whatever happened to the five-second rule? Today, in the name of slovenliness, you are going to forgo the most sacred of cleaning rituals: washing your hands.

The first word that comes to mind, quite naturally, is *gross*. But think about all the harm caused by constant handwashing. Without exposure to germs, your body is completely unprepared should one sneak through. By skipping the suds, you can fortify yourself against an attack.

Go about your normal day, but avoid soap at all costs. Not before you eat, not after you sneeze, not even after you use the bathroom. If you can't resist the urge to wash up, run your hands under some hot water for a few seconds. Just steer clear of anything with the word *sanitizer* on the label. You really don't want a substance that kills 99.9 percent of anything that close to your skin.

PRO TIP

Revert to the fist bump as
your greeting of choice.

Become a Parking Meter Vigilante

"The early bird gets a parking spot and the next guy gets a ticket…that's how it works for us, unfortunately."
—Gary Cunningham, college basketball coach

Sometimes it seems like everyone's out to get you when you're driving a car. If it's not a disgruntled cop ticketing you for disobeying the speed limit, it's a cyclist cutting you off or a pedestrian playing Frogger outside of a crosswalk. But the worst of all are meter maids. They have one goal and one goal only: to ruin a driver's day. Why not save them the pleasure and put money in your fellow drivers' expired meters?

If possible, wait until a meter maid is approaching. Lean nonchalantly against an expired meter, and when the villain whips out a ticketing pad, watch that smug smile fade away as you slip a quarter into the meter. Sure, you'll have made one enemy, but your fellow drivers will consider you a superhero.

Not only are you preventing someone's day from being ruined, but you're also making someone's day. A quarter is worth much more than twenty-five cents when it saves someone a $25 ticket.

PRO TIP

The ticket is recorded the second the maid's pen hits the paper, so make sure to get there before that happens.

Follow an Ambulance Through Traffic

"I stop and look at traffic accidents. I won't hang around, but when I hear something is terrible, as bad as it is, I've gotta look at it."
—Norman Lear, TV producer

Drive at night one time, and you'll notice something strange. The commute is a little smoother and quicker. There aren't as many cars on the road. You're not cursing out the window or at yourself as much. Traffic, it seems, doesn't exist.

It's a lovely sight in contrast to your rush hour commute, when it takes an hour to move a mile.

But there are certain cars that are granted the privilege to pass through traffic whenever they want. They're called ambulances, and all they have to do is turn on their signal and cars get out of their way, no matter how crowded the streets are. It's high time you take advantage of this and just follow the ambulance through traffic. Nobody is going to be later because of it, and the cars behind you will have one less car to worry about since you'll be zooming up ahead of the pack.

It might get you some honks and dirty looks, but at least you'll get home in time to watch the *NCIS* marathon.

PRO TIP

Stay close to the ambulance
or risk getting stuck back
in traffic.

Disorganize Your Desk

*"If a cluttered desk is the sign of a cluttered mind,
what is the significance of a clean desk?"*
—Laurence J. Peter, educator

There's a lot to be said for a clean workspace. It shows your coworkers that you are organized, efficient, and ready to take on whatever tasks come your way. But if spotless living isn't really your strong suit, it can be a difficult front to maintain.

As long as you get your work done on time, it shouldn't matter if you have a few stray candy wrappers floating around and haven't rinsed your coffee mug since March. If anything, a messy desk reflects how hard you've been working. A busy worker doesn't have time to straighten up.

This afternoon, instead of organizing your paper clips according to size and color, you're going to make it look like a tornado hit your cubicle. Unroll the tape dispenser and throw a few wads of tape around your computer. Empty the contents of your junk drawer and scatter them about your workspace. A few empty coffee cups, some random printouts, and a collection of sticky notes later, and you'll look like the busiest (albeit grossest) person in the company. Finally, after years of pretending to be an anal-retentive neat freak, you can embrace the slob you were born to be. Feels good to be yourself, doesn't it?

PRO TIP

Don't do any permanent damage to your space.
You still have to work there tomorrow.

Convert Your Living Room Into a Ball Pit

"When my kids become wild and unruly, I use a nice, safe playpen. When they're finished, I climb out."

—Erma Bombeck, humorist

There's little doubt that McDonald's success would be a fraction of what it is now were it not for the ball pit employed at many of its locations. When you were a child, the sight of a pool of small multicolored plastic balls was like a magnet. You just dropped everything and ran. Even as an adult, you have some longing for those simpler times. So get back in touch with your younger self and convert your living room into a ball pit.

You'd be surprised how easy it is. Internet retailers sell plastic balls used for ball pits. Order ten times as many as you think you need. When your delivery comes, just start unwrapping the bags and bags of balls until they're above your head. Then let your imagination run wild. Your own ball pit is a way to construct a fantasy world. It's also like having your own swimming pool, but one you can walk around in underwater without drowning. Invite your friends over and have a ball pit party. Play tag. Throw the balls at each other. You just became the envy of every child who lives on your block.

PRO TIP

Have a cell phone handy for when you get trapped and need to call for help.

Have Sex in a Library

"I have always imagined that Paradise will be a kind of library."
—Jorge Luis Borges, Argentinian writer and poet

Libraries are truly underappreciated resources. Most have air-conditioning to escape the summer heat, free Wi-Fi to browse the Internet, and all the books you could hope to read in a lifetime of lazy Sundays. Best of all, since almost nobody uses them, you can pretty much do anything you want between the bookshelves. That's right—anything.

Doing the nasty in public is a popular fantasy, but the risk of getting caught is too much for most people. The library solves this problem quite nicely as you are just as likely to get caught bumping uglies in the travel and leisure section of the library as you are in your own bedroom.

The next time you have to return some overdue books, grab your partner and head to the least trafficked area of any library—the history section. Take a look around to make sure nobody's watching, and get down to business as discreetly as possible. Just be sure to keep any moans of ecstasy to a whisper. You're in a library, after all.

PRO TIP

Before you get your groove on, send the librarian on a fool's errand to search for a book that doesn't exist. It'll buy you some much-needed sexy time.

OTHER DISCREET PUBLIC OPTIONS

- Hiking trails
- Empty subway car
- Beach at night
- Golf course after hours

Claim a Store-Bought Dish Is Homemade

"I was thirty-two when I started cooking; up until then, I just ate."
—Julia Child, chef and writer

People love organizing potlucks. Sure, some may view them as an opportunity for their guests to show off their favorite new dish or impress everyone with their best family recipe. But let's call them what they really are: an excuse for the organizer to shirk some of the party planning responsibility. In other words, it's a cop-out. So next time you're invited to a potluck, bring a dish that you made at home—if your home is a grocery store.

The key to pulling this off is getting rid of the evidence before you arrive at the party. Remove the wrapping and trade in the black plastic tray for something from your cabinet.

When you arrive at the party, expect compliments on your picture-perfect dessert. There will undoubtedly be one guest who tries to call your bluff but thinly veils it in a compliment by saying it tastes just like his favorite childhood store-bought baked good. Just tell him it must have been all the time and energy you put into it—then scoff at his lowbrow taste in snacks.

PRO TIP

People will ask for the recipe, so either memorize one you've found in a cookbook or food magazine, or just say, "Oh, it's an old family recipe. My mom would kill me if I told anyone!"

Go to a Strip Club

"I think onstage nudity is disgusting, shameful, and damaging to all things American. But if I were twenty-two with a great body, it would be artistic, tasteful, patriotic, and a progressive religious experience."
—Shelley Winters, actress

Maybe you don't want to be "that guy." Maybe you're a woman and worry you'd look out of place. Or maybe you're a die-hard feminist (male or female) and feel strip clubs are terribly degrading. Whatever the reason, it's time for you to go out and experience the bizarre joy of the strip club—if only just this once.

Now we're not saying all strip clubs are created equal. Some are frightening places that attract the basest levels of humanity. Skip those. But plenty of clubs are surprisingly nice and even what you might call "classy joints," making them ideal places to spend a leisurely evening surrounded by well-proportioned women who just happen to take their clothes off. And contrary to popular belief, women are always welcome. In fact, some dancers claim they're the best tippers. So man or woman, gather some friends and some dollar bills and go make an evening of it. Whether or not you stay true to your original opinion of these sordid contributors to American entertainment, it's worth going to see what they're all about. And if you find yourself enjoying the experience, even better.

PRO TIP

Bring only as much cash as you're willing to spend.
Men and women alike have been known to get
carried away with the tipping.

Hire a Hot Personal Trainer

"The word aerobics *came about when the gym instructors got together and said, 'If we're going to charge $10 an hour, we can't call it jumping up and down.'"*

—Rita Rudner, comedian

New Year's has come and gone, and with it so, too, has your New Year's resolution to get in shape. Nothing you do can keep your motivation up—even when you reward yourself with a sip of beer after each sit-up. Those sips of beer became more frequent, and the sit-ups less so. The fact is if you don't have a reason to go to the gym, you're not going to go. And therefore you have no choice but to hire a hot personal trainer.

It shouldn't be hard. Most personal trainers are young, in shape, and pretty hot. Are they qualified? If they can get themselves to look like that, then they must know something. But just to be sure, you should conduct an extensive interview process. Once you select the right candidate, you'll find yourself dreaming about going to the gym all day. Suddenly that motivation problem is solved.

PRO TIP

If you find your personal trainer is getting too hot during your workout, go-to thoughts can include Grandma's cookies, baseball, and the comedy stylings of Bill Maher.

BUYER BEWARE

A 2002 investigation of the modern world of personal trainers found that 70 percent of those surveyed did not have a degree in any field related to exercise science.

Blast Awful Music in Traffic

"There are two kinds of music: German music and bad music."
—H.L. Mencken, writer

Aside from running on a treadmill, sitting in traffic may very well be the most dreadful experience known to man—nothing but you, your brake pedal, and a sea of angry motorists as far as the eye can see.

A little guilty pleasure music should help pass the time. Normally you'd play it at a whisper to spare your fellow motorists from your awful taste in music, but not this time. Today you're going to crank your crappy tunes as loud as they'll go, and everyone else will just have to deal with it. If they didn't want to listen to Justin Bieber's greatest Christmas hits, then hey, they shouldn't have taken the expressway.

PRO TIP

Be prepared to roll up the windows to deflect flying coffee cups and tomatoes.

Sit Around
in Your Underwear

"I wasn't really naked. I simply didn't have any clothes on."
—Josephine Baker, actress

Back in your bygone childhood years, the majority of your time was likely spent in nothing more than Mickey Mouse or Barbie underpants. But now that you're an adult, modesty (and often the law) compels you to cover up for daily activities. But imagine your normal activities without the excess clothes: no collars or sleeves to restrict you, no fabric to adjust, no tight waist to battle. Just you, the open air, and your skivvies—sounds great, right?

Bring back the underwear mode and spend your time at home sans clothing. Try whipping up some pasta carbonara while sipping a glass of wine, or spend some hours sprawled on the couch for a movie marathon, all in your Underoos. If anyone stops by for an unexpected visit, resist the urge to cover up. Instead, greet your friend with the stiffest poker face you can muster and ask the person to join you. Your visitor will find it either really liberating—or really weird.

PRO TIP

When you're cooking in the kitchen, throw on an apron to protect all that bare skin from splattering grease.

Fake a Headache So You Can Just Go to Sleep

"And then Adam said, 'What's a headache?'"
—Unknown

It happens to everyone—you climb into bed after a long day, feel your significant other's suggestive hand on your thigh, and think, *Do we really have to do this tonight?* Most evenings you would succumb to your S.O.'s advances to keep things on an even keel, but tonight you want to sleep, and dammit, you're going to sleep.

So instead of acquiescing, put on your best "I don't feel good" face, rub your temples a few times, and gently tell your partner that since your head has been hurting all day, you need to sleep it off instead of engaging in any strenuous activity. If there's a fuss, kiss your partner a few times and promise a rollicking bedtime session tomorrow night.

There may be pouting for a few minutes, but rest assured a night will come when your partner does the exact same thing to you. So for tonight, ditch the guilt and get to sleep.

PRO TIP
....

Keep a bottle of pain reliever
by the bed so you can take
some as part of your "I have a
headache" scheme.

Sneak Onto a Golf Course

"Although golf was originally restricted to wealthy, overweight Protestants, today it's open to anybody who owns hideous clothing."
—Dave Barry, humorist

If you want to play on the best courses in the world, a single round of golf can set you back hundreds of dollars—unless, of course, you are willing to be a little sneaky.

Take a look around a golf course and notice what isn't there: fences, security guards, attack dogs, alarm systems. There is literally nothing to prevent you from hopping on for free, aside from a few pimple-faced caddies and your own conscience.

What are you waiting for?

Throw on your ugliest pair of plaid shorts, grab your clubs, and head to the links. If you act confident and tee off straight away, nobody is going to question your legitimacy as a paying customer. If it's a fancier course, staff members may even treat you to some free drinks or a nice cigar while you swindle them out of a free round of golf.

PRO TIP

The first hole is usually right next to the clubhouse, so skip over to the second or third to avoid detection.

Go Uncamping

"Some national parks have long waiting lists for camping reservations. When you have to wait a year to sleep next to a tree, something is wrong."
—George Carlin, comedian

Ah, camping—the sweet sting of mosquitoes, the fragrant aroma of canned beans, the intrinsic joy of burying your own waste.

Screw roughing it. Next time your loved ones ask you to join them in the wild, tell them you'll go uncamping instead. Bring a generator and a portable air conditioner. Pack your laptop and a week's worth of DVDs. Cram a king-sized air mattress and a beanbag chair into your deluxe three-room tent. Tuck champagne and tins of caviar into the cooler next to the hot dogs and beer. Or better yet, make arrangements to have a pizza delivered straight to the campsite.

After all, there's no reason to separate yourself from nature. Some of us just prefer to combine it with our other loves—like our PlayStation.

PRO TIP

To avoid any al fresco fist-fights, be sure to set up your uncamping campsite out of earshot of anyone looking for peace and quiet.

Fake an Impressive Life

"I'd like to live as a poor man with lots of money."
—Pablo Picasso, artist

It's date night, and there's only one thing standing between you and some wild post-date hanky-panky: the messy, cluttered hole-in-the-wall that you call home. While you can't change your station in life overnight, you can at least fake it for a few hours.

Check your local real estate listings and track down an upscale loft in the trendy, hip part of town—bonus points if it has a hot tub, a dance floor, an indoor basketball hoop, or access to a rooftop pool. Explain to the real estate agent that you're interested in buying, but you'd like to spend the night to get a feel for the place.

Now all that's left is to go back to your swinging pad and watch as your date's jaw drops to the floor—which is made out of rare canary wood, by the way.

PRO TIP

If you'll be drinking, hire a chauffeur to drive you and your date home. It will complete the illusion.

MOST EXPENSIVE REAL ESTATE

- Monaco: $6,550 per square foot
- London: $3,670 per square foot
- New York City: $2,160 per square foot
- Moscow: $2,120 per square foot

Start a Fight
Just for the Makeup Sex

"Sex is emotion in motion."
—Mae West, actress

Fights are an inevitability in any relationship. If you spend enough time with somebody, there's going to be the occasional disagreement. The good news is that the more bitter the dispute, the more heated and passionate the reconciliation.

Alas, you haven't had a fight in months, but don't despair. Just because you and your partner are getting along better than ever doesn't mean you have to miss out on mind-blowing makeup sex. It's time to stir things up a little.

When you greet your significant other tonight, come prepared with a list of pet peeves and complaints, and bombard your S.O. with everything you've got. Don't let up until your S.O. storms out in a fit of rage. After you've both had a while to cool down, lay on the apologies. Once everything's smoothed over, it's time to attack one another with the reckless abandon only a truly epic fight can engender. Sure, it's a little manipulative, but your partner certainly won't be complaining when it's over.

PRO TIP

Don't take it too far, or you
could be sleeping on the
couch—or on the street—
instead of in your lover's arms.

Claim an Empty Office

*"It is better to take what does not belong to you
than to let it lie around neglected."*
—Mark Twain, writer

Layoffs are hard on everyone. Layoffs have also left a couple of empty offices around your workplace. Every day you peer in and wonder if the company is gonna use that space for anything. It's been two months. Your cubicle mates are constantly sniffling, coughing, and playing their radios without headphones. You deserve to claim that empty office as your own.

Move your stuff in early, before work starts. Get your computer set up, put up some family photos, move your chair in, and lean back. It's best to move in and then tell your superior that the CEO told you that you could take any open office space until it was needed. It gives you an alibi, and if the company needs the space, you look inconvenienced more than anything else. Once you establish yourself there over time, the office will slowly become your property. Then you can slowly expand your empire by annexing adjacent offices and desks. But it's best to exercise patience. Don't look too far ahead.

PRO TIP

Leave some papers and folders on your old desk so it doesn't look completely abandoned. It may throw people off for some time while you establish your presence in your new office.

THINGS TO DO
IN YOUR OWN OFFICE

• Decorate it as you please
• Look out upon the peons
• Listen to your music with the door closed
• Sleep under your desk
• Fart to your heart's content

Bike Without a Helmet

*"Believe me! The secret of reaping the greatest fruitfulness and the
greatest enjoyment from life is to live dangerously!"*
—Friedrich Nietzsche, German philosopher

There are many great things about biking. It's environmentally friendly,
efficient, fun, and inexpensive. Too bad you have to wear an oversized salad
bowl on your head in order to ride one.

Sure, a helmet can save your life, but it's also uncomfortable, hot, and
ridiculously stupid-looking. They're fine for uncoordinated children and
the elderly, but not for someone as graceful and athletic as yourself. It's only
protecting your brain, and how much were you really using that, anyway?

Today, instead of delicately balancing pounds of plastic on your
cranium, leave your helmet in the garage where it belongs. Feel the wind
whipping through your hair as you fly down hills and zip in and out of
traffic.

Since you don't have a helmet to block your view, take in the gorgeous
scenery as you ride—but not for too long. You don't want to fall and hit
your head—it's surprisingly fragile without protective gear.

PRO TIP

Keep it under 10 miles per
hour, or learn to fall on your
feet.

HELMET ALTERNATIVES

- Turban
- Saucepan
- Plastic bucket
- Sponges and a belt

Assume a Fake Identity

*"We are what we pretend to be,
so we must be careful about what we pretend to be."*
—Kurt Vonnegut, writer

No matter how comfortable you are with yourself, wouldn't it be fun to be someone else, even if just for a day? Why not go for it?

Buy a wig. Find nonprescription cat's-eye glasses. Style your hair in a brand-new way. Wear red lipstick. Become that guy who dons seersucker suits and carries a cane, or that woman who sports pink wigs and sparkly eye shadow. Adopt an accent. Assume a new name—a fun one—and introduce yourself enthusiastically wherever you go.

After all, this is textbook acting, and there are no limits on the person you can become. You might even like the new you so much that you decide to let your alter ego stick around indefinitely.

PRO TIP

Be sure you've carefully internalized your new name so you don't give yourself away by not responding to it.

FUN ALTERNATE-IDENTITY NAMES

- Veronica
- Beatrix
- Svetlana
- Claude
- Engelbert
- Thor

Pass a Forgery Off as an Original Painting

"Bad artists copy. Good artists steal."

—Pablo Picasso, artist

When you see a famous painting hanging on someone's wall, you can't help but admire their sense of good taste and envy their ability to afford such indulgences. It certainly makes you wish you could trade in your family portraits for something a little classier.

But just because you can't afford expensive art doesn't mean you don't deserve a nicely decorated wall. Instead of waiting to save up thousands of dollars to purchase an original, perhaps you can settle for the next best thing: a clever forgery. For a fraction of the price of an authentic painting, you can purchase a respectable re-creation online.

Once you get it home, you can concoct an elaborate story to explain its presence in your humble home. Perhaps your great-uncle was an art dealer. Maybe your parents found it beneath the floorboards in their attic. If you invest in an expensive frame and stick to your story, nobody will ever know your sinful secret.

PRO TIP

Pick relatively obscure artists to display. People are less likely to spot the forgery if the painting isn't famous.

ALTERNATIVE OPTIONS

- Finger painting (modern art)
- Newspaper collage (contemporary art)
- Empty frame (existential art)

Crash a Lunch Meeting

"People who enjoy meetings should not be in charge of anything."
—Thomas Sowell, writer

Lunchtime rolls around, and the egg salad sandwich you brought is about as appetizing as the bag in which you packed it. Suddenly you have a ray of hope as the familiar scent of takeout wafts from the conference room.

You may not have been invited to the meeting directly, but you would be doing the company a disservice if you didn't attend. If you don't offer your expert opinion, countless minutes could be lost talking in circles. Quietly sneak into the meeting room and grab a seat close to the lunch food. While you stuff your face, jot down a few notes and mumble in agreement so you look like you belong there. As long as you keep your head down, nobody will even notice you are there. It will be just like every other meeting you've ever been to.

PRO TIP

If anybody asks you a direct question—like what you're doing there—pretend to choke on some Szechuan chicken and head for the nearest exit.

OFFICE JARGON TRANSLATED

- Synergy: Pawning off work on another department
- Action item: Something we forgot to do
- Deadline: An utterly meaningless, arbitrary date

Organize a Cool-Kids Table in the Lunchroom

"Now if you break any of these rules, you can't sit with us at lunch.
I mean, not just you. Like, any of us. Okay, like, if I was wearing jeans
today, I would be sitting over there with the art freaks. Oh, and we
always vote before we ask someone to eat lunch with us because
you have to be considerate of the rest of the group."
—*Gretchen Wieners*, Mean Girls

A quick scan of the lunchroom yields your typical mix of groups—the geeks, the goody-goodies, the antisocial people, and the weirdos. You seriously don't fit in with any of those people, so there's only one thing left to do: start a cool-kids table. Clearly it's just as necessary in real life as it was in high school.

First, identify your cool coworkers—typically they will be around your age and would certainly not be wearing something weird like elasticized pants or a beret. Next, figure out what time you should eat. Avoid the noon to 1:00 p.m. crunch because the lunchroom will be filled and you'll get hangers-on to your group. Finally, tell your selected colleagues and make it happen.

With a cool-kids table in place, you'll look forward to lunch hour even more than you already do. And *that* is something to celebrate.

PRO TIP
....

Continue going out to lunch one or two times a week
to maintain your cool-kids aura of mystery.

Start a Pillow Fight in Public

"We just want to inspire girls to have pillow fights and then drive to the beach and break up with their boyfriends!"
—Ben Romans, composer

Let's face it: pillow fights are awesome. Everyone gets to unleash their repressed aggression, and nobody gets hurt. So why must they be relegated to children's sleepovers and sorority houses? Today you can bring the pillow fight to the mainstream by staging an epic battle in public.

Head to your nearest department store and buy out every pillow it has. Now take your arsenal to the streets, wait for unsuspecting commuters to start heading to work, and start smacking. Be direct, aim true, and strike hard. Be as aggressive as possible without causing any real physical harm.

It shouldn't take long for everyone to figure out what's going on and grab some pillows from your pile to join in. Sure, they may be a few minutes late to work, but they'll have the most fun morning commute ever.

PRO TIP

Don't attack anyone holding coffee or wearing glasses. It's just mean.

PILLOWS FOR EVERYONE!

The largest pillow fight flash mob took place during the International Pillow Fight Day on March 22, 2008.

Toilet-Paper a House the Night Before Halloween

"Today you can go to a gas station and find the cash register open and the toilets locked. They must think toilet paper is worth more than money."
—Joey Bishop, actor and comedian

If a teacher, fellow student, or parent offended your sensibilities when you were young, you did the brave thing. You teamed up with your friends, bought sixteen rolls of toilet paper, and anonymously TP'd the offending party's house. The person then knew he had violated some kind of social code and had to hang his head in shame as the neighborhood snickered at him behind his back.

Get back in touch with your inner child and TP a house this Halloween. You had so much fun doing it as a child. It was a beautiful combination of fear and righteous indignation. Now that you're older and have dignity, the fear factor will be even higher. Plus, the decoration goes well with the holiday. It makes the tree look like it's celebrating along with everyone else. So join in the fun this holiday season and let the toilet paper fly.

PRO TIP
....

Wear dark clothing and do
the TP thing at night.

Cheat on Your Taxes

"When there's a single thief, it's robbery.
When there are a thousand thieves, it's taxation."
—Vanya Cohen, musician

Every year we do the same song and dance with the government. We make money, and the government wants some of it. Naturally we don't want to give it away. What's a law-abiding American citizen to do? This year do what you've always wanted to do. Cheat on your taxes.

Actually *cheat* is a strong word. Massage your taxes. Luckily the government gives us all a chance to hide our money. First, open a PO box in Bermuda. We're not sure how this will help exactly, but it can't hurt. Also, that dining room table you just bought? Work expense. You've thought about work while sitting there, right? No? Doesn't matter, it's tax-deductible. Also, your pet dog can technically be considered a dependent since it relies on you for food, drink, and love. Actually, by that metric, so is the stray cat in the alleyway. All of a sudden, *cha-ching*. You've got a big tax refund coming your way. And you're risking only a multiyear prison sentence to get it!

PRO TIP

If you're caught, just claim it was your tax preparer's fault.

Splurge on Useless Gadgets

"A new gadget that lasts only five minutes is worth more than an immortal work that bores everyone."
—Francis Picabia, artist

There was a time when your bulky laptop and flimsy flip phone were innovative pieces of technology. Now they're about as state-of-the-art as a fountain pen.

Your outdated electronics still technically work, but think of all the faster, sleeker gadgets out there that you could be enjoying. Splurging on flashy new technology might not be the most economical decision you make all day, but it will be the coolest. Run, don't walk, to your local gadget emporium and stock up on top-of-the-line computers, smartphones, and home theater equipment. Heck, even pick up a few luxury items you don't even need, like an automatic wine opener or an electric towel warmer.

Take your new gadgets and bask in the glory of owning all state-of-the-art equipment. You've got a solid six months before they are completely obsolete.

PRO TIP

Research your gadgets online to ensure you are buying the most state-of-the-art models.

BEST GADGET STORES

- The Sharper Image
- Hammacher Schlemmer
- Best Buy

Pretend to Be a Student

"College is the best time of your life. When else are your parents going to spend several thousand dollars a year just for you to go to a strange town and get drunk every night?"
—David Wood, actor and writer

Remember college? Four years of keg stands, unlimited dining hall food, and Frisbee on the quad punctuated with the occasional philosophy class. Compared to your current daily itinerary of mindless cubicle work, peewee soccer games, family dinners, and reruns of *Seinfeld*, college was a veritable paradise.

Although you can't travel back in time to your glory days in college, you can travel to your nearest institution of higher learning to relive them. You may be several years (or decades) older than the average student, but that doesn't mean that you can't still keep up with them.

Once you are on campus, take this opportunity to sneak into a large lecture hall and actually pay attention—to make up for all the years you spent falling asleep in class. If the weather's nice, there's sure to be a protest or two going on that you can join. If you play the part right, everyone will just assume you're an aging grad student—and you might even get invited to a kegger.

PRO TIP

Be sure to bring along a backpack and $2 flip-flops to blend in.

Deep-Fry Everything

"I was never usually squeamish; I could sometimes eat a fried rat with a good relish, if it was necessary."
—Henry David Thoreau, writer and philosopher

Many people overlook the fact that deep-frying an item—regardless of its flavor profile—increases its deliciousness by a power of ten. Don't believe it? Think about the following gustatory delights:

- **Macaroni and cheese:** Check.

- **Pickles:** Check.

- **Ice cream:** Double check.

Sadly only a fraction of the average diet consists of fried food. Such a shame—all that flavor-enhancing power sacrificed in the name of a thin waistline.

Not you, though. You're perfectly happy the way you are. And just imagine how happy you'll be once you deep-fry everything in your kitchen. So tie on your apron, heat a few quarts of oil in a Dutch oven, prepare some batter, and throw in whatever you can find. Sweet foods like candy bars, fruit, cookies, and brownies work great, but don't forget more offbeat savory items like olives, eggs, and pizza.

PRO TIP

Cook sweet and savory foods in separate oil.
Otherwise your deep-fried Oreos might taste
like fish sticks.

Pretend to Be Single
for the Day

"When they are alone they want to be with others, and when they are with others they want to be alone. After all, human beings are like that."
—Gertrude Stein, writer

When you were single, you claimed to love every minute of it. The freedom! The possibilities! The opportunity to pee with the door open! Of course, now that you're in a relationship, you can finally stop worrying about dying alone. Really you're happier this way. So why is it starting to seem like so much...work?

You know what you need? A Single Day. Take a day and don't do anything except what you want to do. Don't take any calls from your significant other—admit it's not on your list of priorities to hear about work conflicts or the long wait for the train. Go for a two-hour run, or sit on the couch and take in a marathon of the trashy reality shows your loved one refuses to watch. Make dinner plans with your friends, or devour an entire box of macaroni and cheese without fear of judgment.

Because just as taking a vacation day makes work more bearable, a Single Day gives you the energy you need to be in a relationship—happily.

PRO TIP

Make sure you've informed your significant other that you're taking a Single Day. Otherwise twenty-four hours of radio silence may make returning to your relationship more difficult than you thought.

Waste Gas and Go for a Sunday Drive

"A driver is a king on a vinyl bucket-seat throne, changing direction with the turn of a wheel, changing the climate with a flick of the button, changing the music with the switch of a dial."
—Andrew H. Malcolm, writer

Gas prices are climbing, which has put a damper on travel plans that don't involve bicycle spokes or your own two legs.

But you know what? Sundays are for three things: sleeping in, brunch, and leisurely drives. So this Sunday, forget the prices at the pump and get behind that wheel. Wherever you live, chances are there's some beautiful scenery just an hour or two away—mountains or rivers, grassy plains or sandy beaches, covered bridges or horse-dotted pastures. After all, there's nothing better than zooming down a country road on a summer afternoon with the windows down and the stereo up. So sleep in, eat that brunch, and get driving.

PRO TIP

If you spring for the Bloody Mary at brunch, line up an alternate driver. The scenery's even better from the passenger seat.

DRIVE YOUR CARES AWAY

Automobile pioneer Henry Ford was an advocate of the Sunday drive. Though many Christians observe Sunday as a day of rest, he promoted it as a day of activity to generate more automobile sales.

Crank Up the A/C

"No pleasure, no rapture, no exquisite sin greater...than central air."
—Azrael, Dogma

Environmental advocates are everywhere these days, and they have the blue and green bins to prove it. Not only are they forcing us all to reduce, reuse, and recycle, but now they're on a rampage to curb global warming, and our beloved air conditioners are on the chopping block.

This aggression will not stand. It's time to take up arms against your eco-friendly foes by wantonly wasting energy today. Crank every air conditioner in your house until it's a frosty 50 degrees and you have to throw on a sweater to keep the goosebumps at bay. If your A/C units are struggling to keep up, crack open your freezer for some extra cool air. Peel back the blinds and watch as hordes of sweaty tree huggers swelter in the boiling sun. Just be thankful it isn't you, and pour yourself another mug of hot cocoa in the comfort of your chilly sanctuary.

PRO TIP

Just remember this is a one-day indulgence. You can't afford to live in a temperature-controlled bio-dome forever.

CHEAPER WAYS TO COOL DOWN

- Place a block of ice next to your fan
- Keep the blinds closed
- Order delivery instead of turning on the oven
- Leave all the lights off

Fake an Injury to Cut the Amusement Park Lines

"Success has always been a great liar."
—Friedrich Nietzsche, German philosopher

The thing about amusement parks is that it's quite unamusing to wait forty minutes in line for a ride. If you want your thrills to be timely, you're stuck with the kiddie ride that creeps along at two miles an hour. By the time you get to the front of the seven-loop roller coaster line, the park is about to close.

Aside from buying those expensive member passes, it is possible to skip the lines by milking sympathy and feigning a hobble. Or a broken wrist. Or a sprained toe. When you're injured, you get to jump to the front with everyone's blessing.

Warm up those acting skills for your next park visit, and get that spot in line you've always wanted. A prop is key, so make sure you've got a pair of crutches or a sling. (Who knew that old bike injury would come in handy?) Better yet, grab a wheelchair from the welcome center. With a few pitiful looks, you should be ushered to the front and having the ride of your life.

PRO TIP

Pick an injury that's not too serious. You want to be allowed to ride, after all.

Steal Office Supplies
from Work

"Y—excuse me. You—I believe you have my stapler?"
—*Milton Waddams,* Office Space

How many times have you been at home and realized that you desperately need but do not have paper clips, a stapler, envelopes, or all of the above? Somehow office supplies never seem to make it onto your grocery list, so you might as well just quit trying. The solution is simple: steal them from work.

Companies across the country are awash in office supplies, from three-ring binders to tape dispensers. Supplies are available for employee use, so if you're an employee, help yourself! That's not to say you should cart out whole boxes of stuff, but surely no one will miss a Post-it cube here or a ruler there.

Don't even think of it as stealing. Instead, consider your little office supplies caper as "utilizing the resources your company provides to the fullest extent." Even HR can't argue with that.

PRO TIP

Appropriate your goodies either before or after work to minimize your chances of being caught.

REVENGE IS SWEET

A recent OfficeMax survey revealed that six in ten Americans have stolen office supplies from work to use at home. Not surprisingly, pens, pencils, and highlighters were the most commonly pilfered items.

Walk Around in a Bathrobe All Day

"I don't want to look like a weirdo.
I'll just go with the muumuu."
—*Homer Simpson,* The Simpsons

You may have yourself convinced that your work clothes are perfectly comfortable, but let's face it: your comfiest suit doesn't even hold a candle to your bathrobe. It seems kind of silly that you wear your most luxurious garment for only a few minutes each day. Just this once, you're going to get a little more use out of it.

When you get out of the shower, reach for your cushiest bathrobe and wrap yourself in its warm, soothing embrace. Instead of treating it as a piece of transition clothing, wear it around and go about your life as normal. Walk the dog, run errands, head to yoga class—all in the comfort and style of a robe.

Better yet, go to dinner and/or drinks in the robe, ignoring any protests by front-of-house staff. Smoke cigars and read the paper as you see fit. If anyone asks why you're wearing a bathrobe in public, just roll your eyes and keep on strutting. Haters gonna hate.

PRO TIP

Secure your robe tightly
or risk flashing the entire
restaurant.

Steal Your Neighbor's Flowers

*"Flowers are the sweetest things God ever made
and forgot to put a soul into."*
—Henry Ward Beecher, writer

You can't be bothered with such trivial things as planting flowers or tending to a garden. That takes a level of effort that you're just not willing to give. Your neighbor, however, is a regular Martha Stewart. She's out there every morning on her knees, weeding the beds and spreading mulch. At night she dutifully soaks the ground with a garden hose. The result of all her effort is a garden teeming with life in a variety of colors and shapes.

Be honest: it actually looks nice. You're a little jealous of those flowers, aren't you? Kind of wish you'd planted some of your own, after all? When your neighbor is out, sneak over into her yard and snip off a few blossoms to enjoy in your own home. Arrange them artfully in a vase and admire all the hard work that went into growing them. Then pat yourself on the back since you weren't the one who had to do it.

PRO TIP

Don't cut so many flowers that she'll notice they're gone. Instead, go for a more random, mixed bouquet approach—one flower here, another flower there—and she won't suspect a thing.

WHAT DIFFERENT COLOR-ED ROSES MEAN

- Red: Love and romance
- Pink: Admiration and appreciation
- Yellow: Friendship
- White: Remembrance
- Lavender: Love at first sight

Crack Open an Expensive Bottle of Wine to Celebrate a Mundane Achievement

"Life is too short to drink bad wine."

—Unknown

Wouldn't it be nice if you felt as though you accomplished something magnificent every day? Like that time you successfully passed the CPA exam or the day you got engaged. Unfortunately you're not going to do something fantastic every day, but that doesn't mean you can't kick up your heels anyway.

Everyone knows life is more fun when you have something to celebrate, so go ahead and turn one of your most mundane "achievements" into a splurge-worthy occasion. Filed your taxes on time? Crack open that bottle of Dom Pérignon stashed behind your cheap vodka. Took your dog to the vet for her checkup? Treat yourself to the vintage bottle of Barolo that Grandma gave you as a college graduation present.

Let's face it: not all of us are going to win the Nobel Prize or invent the next *Facebook*. So we might as well just break open a bottle of bubbly to celebrate a mundane achievement that says, "I'm here and I'm not a failure."

PRO TIP

Be careful not to hit yourself in the face if you're uncorking a bottle of champagne.

Start a Snowball Fight

"The aging process has you firmly in its grasp
if you never get the urge to throw a snowball."
—Doug Larson, journalist

During your entire childhood, you were constantly kept from starting a snowball fight. "Put the snowball down!" you were told. "Don't you dare!"

Well, you're an adult now. And if there's one thing that persists even after you've entered adulthood, it's that little devil on your shoulder telling you to do the opposite of what you're told. So go on and start the snowball fight you never got to initiate when you were a kid.

It's important to establish yourself as a force to be reckoned with early on. So take risks: do a sniper roll to get behind that tree. Expose yourself from behind that snowdrift if it means getting a better shot at your opponent.

Sure, you should probably be shoveling the snow instead of packing it into balls. But where's the fun in that? After all, the best part of being an adult is acting like a kid.

PRO TIP

Don't pull the old "rock in the snowball" trick. Remember that you're an adult now—and you'll be tried as one.

BEST HIDING PLACES IN A SNOWBALL FIGHT

- In a tree
- Behind a civilian
- Under a (parked) car
- In a snowman
- On top of a building (sniper-style)

Give Zero Weeks' Notice

"The best way to appreciate your job
is to imagine yourself without one."
—Oscar Wilde, writer

Have you ever sat behind your desk at a job where you're underpaid and underappreciated and imagined reenacting job-quitting scenes like those in movies such as *American Beauty, Fight Club,* and *Office Space*? If so, it's time you made your daydream a reality.

There's no need to think about your post-quitting plans. The only thing to consider is how to make your kiss-off the most memorable your office has ever seen—though neglecting to give the requisite two weeks is in itself probably going to earn you firm standing in the company's quitting history.

Giving your boss a two-week cushion is for suckers. You've been a subordinate for as long as you've had the job. Now it's time to become the boss of your biggest work project yet: quitting. You wanted to do something, so you went and did it. When you get home, make sure to add "go-getter" to your resume.

PRO TIP

On your way out, don't do anything illegal like break a computer or hurt a coworker. Those things are fun only in the movies, where there are no consequences.

Take an Hour-Long Shower

"Cleanliness is next to godliness."
—Proverb

Most days when you're getting ready, time is of the essence. Taking a shower is just that thing you have to do before getting dressed, so you're usually in and out of the bathroom in under ten minutes. Rarely do you take your time in there and really savor the experience.

Next time you take a shower, give yourself a full hour to stay under the water. Patiently scrub each toe and wash behind your ears. Use one of those pumice stones on your feet, sloughing away dead skin and thoroughly exfoliating every inch of skin. When was the last time you let your fingers get good and pruned, anyway? Completely lather up before shaving every inch of your body, and then just stand there, doing nothing, for a solid twenty minutes.

When it's time to shampoo your hair, lather, rinse, and then actually repeat. And then again. Bring a radio into the bathroom, and sing along at the top of your lungs while massaging conditioner into your scalp for the third or fourth time.

PRO TIP

Make sure none of your family members or roommates will need the bathroom while you're in there—nothing ruins bath time like someone knocking on the door saying he needs to pee.

Invoke the Five-Second Rule

"If I drop food on the floor, I pick it up and eat it!
Even if I'm at sidewalk cafe! In Calcutta!"
—George Carlin, comedian

When it comes to cooking, there are few tragedies worse than watching all your hard work slowly cascade to the floor. You know you should just throw it away and start from scratch, but is it really worth all the extra effort? Nobody saw you drop it. As long as it didn't land in a pile of pet hair, there's nothing a quick rinse in the sink can't fix.

Don't stop to think about the last time you mopped the floor. Simply grab the remnants of your meal and rearrange it back on the plate. Just remember you may have to sacrifice the portion that actually made contact with the ground if your floor is especially dirty. Or at least make sure nobody is looking before you eat it.

PRO TIP

Blow on your food prior to ingestion. This will kill approximately 0.0 percent of germs.

UNSALVAGEABLE FOODS

- Soup
- Pasta
- Cereal (if you've already added milk)
- Ice cream
- Pudding

Ignore Price Tags

"I buy expensive suits. They just look cheap on me."
—Warren Buffett, investor

This must be how the wealthy live—or at least those with unlimited credit cards. Take yourself out shopping for the day and pay no mind to the number on the price tag. In fact, don't even look at the price tags. When the cashier rings you up at the register, tell her you'd rather not know the total. Just swipe your card and worry about the money later.

When you're not worrying about money, the shopping experience is all about the look and feel of the clothes. Try on elegant ball gowns or sharply cut suits. That cashmere sweater sure does feel nice to the touch. Why not buy two? A different pair of fancy underwear for every day of the year? Sure! When money is no object, no object is off-limits.

PRO TIP

Become familiar with the store's return policy and save all receipts so you can make any necessary returns once the inevitable buyer's remorse sets in.

MAKING EXTRA CASH TO PAY OFF YOUR CREDIT CARD

- Babysit your neighbors' kids
- Donate sperm/eggs
- Sell old books and clothes
- Get a second job bartending at night
- Have a garage sale

Walk Around
Your House Naked

*"My ideal is to wake up in the morning
and run around the meadow naked."*
—Daryl Hannah, actress

When you get home from work, the first thing you probably do is slip into something more comfortable. But when you think about it, what could possibly be more comfortable than nothing at all? When you finish off a hard day, instead of changing into constricting sweatpants, just unzip and let loose. Nobody's watching, so you're free to walk around your house as naked as a jaybird. But don't stop at just strutting around. Clean the place naked, watch TV naked, or even eat a sandwich naked. It's your house, after all; you can do what you want.

It's not even about being sexy; it's just about being comfortable and relaxed. You were born naked, so it's only natural to wander around that way.

PRO TIP

Don't lose sight of your nakedness. If you forget and grab the mail in your birthday suit, you might offend a neighbor or two.

EMERGENCY CLOTHING OPTIONS

- Potted plants
- Lampshade
- A black piece of rectangular construction paper
- Hands

Watch Only Reality TV

"Anyone who relies exclusively on television for his or her knowledge of the world is making a serious mistake."
—Steve Powers, artist

These days television programs fall into one of three categories: news, crime dramas, and reality shows. And there's only one genre worth watching: reality shows.

Let's face it: your friends aren't going to be discussing actual breaking news next time you get together. They're going to be talking about the latest girl fight or love triangle on their favorite reality show, and you need to keep up.

So rebel against those who say reality television is a waste of time and brain cells. They're wrong. On the contrary, it's the best way to stay in the know. So watch reality shows—all of them. You'll be amazed at how quickly you start to feel great about yourself. After all, you've never eaten a twenty-pound burrito right before running a road race in South Africa before giving a rose to the partner of your dreams—at least not yet anyway. And if there's one thing to be learned from reality TV, it's that those who can't do, watch.

PRO TIP

Some people think reality TV is trash, but think of them more as sociological experiments or exercises in how not to live.

Do a Half-Assed Cleaning Job

"My idea of housework is to sweep the room with a glance."
—Erma Bombeck, humorist

You've overlooked the dirty dishes, mountains of dust bunnies, and curiously sticky floors for far too long. If you don't clean up soon, whatever is growing in the fridge might become self-aware and stage a coup.

But let's not get ahead of ourselves here. You certainly do have to tidy up a bit, but nobody ever said you had to go crazy. After all, is there really a difference between something that looks clean and something that is clean?

Instead of vacuuming the carpet—which wasn't really that dirty to begin with—just spray some deodorizer on the ground. That strange smell emanating from the vegetable drawer? Nothing a little baking soda can't fix. And you'd be amazed at how quickly you can mop if you strap sponges to your feet while you walk around.

With the time you've saved cutting corners, you can focus on more important things—like finishing last week's Sunday crossword or watching reruns of *The Bachelorette*.

PRO TIP

Keep your house messy whenever possible. That way small improvements will appear more dramatic.

WASTE OF TIME

Each year the average person spends 657 hours tending to household chores.

Play on a Playground

"The world is a playground, and life is pushing my swing."
—Natalie Kocsis, actress

When you were a kid, there were few things more magical than exploring the local playground. You could spend an entire day hanging on the monkey bars or launching yourself from the swings. Sadly you aren't a kid anymore. Now the closest you get to spinning on the merry-go-round is the two seconds it takes to walk through the revolving door as you enter the office each morning.

But what's stopping you from recapturing your childhood? It's not like there's a force field surrounding all playgrounds that locks out anyone above the age of fourteen. Playgrounds are designed to be played upon. So what are you waiting for?

Run, don't walk, to the nearest playground and head straight for the biggest slide you can find. Climb up and down the cargo net, run the wrong way up the slide, and even play with the stupid giant tic-tac-toe game. Pay no attention to the confused stares of your fellow "adults." They're just jealous.

PRO TIP

Bring a child along so you seem less creepy.

BEST PLAYGROUND GAMES

- Capture the Flag
- The Ground Is Lava
- King of the Hill
- Throw Wood Chips at Each Other and Call It a Game

Watch Movies All Day

"I think cinema, movies, and magic have always been closely associated. The very earliest people who made film were magicians."
—Francis Ford Coppola, movie director

Ah, the weekend: the perfect time to catch up on all the errands and chores you've been neglecting all week. It can be so rewarding to check things off your to-do list. Of course, it can also be rewarding to sit on the couch and watch TV until your eyes bleed.

When was the last time you saw a good movie anyway? Let alone seven good movies back-to-back? Your list of to-dos has taken a back seat for weeks now. It can certainly wait another twenty-four hours while you catch up with your movie collection. Dust off a few of your favorite flicks and plan the ultimate movie marathon. You can create a list of greatest hits, stick entirely to D-rated horror films, or watch an entire movie series in a single afternoon—you've got nothing but time.

PRO TIP

Stockpile popcorn, candy, pizza, and soda to avoid a break in the action.

ULTIMATE MOVIE MARATHONS

- Lord of the Rings trilogy (3 films): 11 hours, 18 minutes
- Star Wars series (10 films): 22 hours, 30 minutes
- Harry Potter series (8 films): 19 hours, 39 minutes

Do a Second Job on Company Time

"You will never 'find' time for anything.
If you want time, you must make it."
—Charles Bruxton, British politician

Everyone wants to find a way to earn a little extra money, and many people have spent years dreaming of opening their own business. Unfortunately self-employment is expensive. It's not likely that you just have a photocopier sitting around at home, after all.

If you're feeling really ambitious, don't hesitate to start your own business on the company dime. You have everything you could possibly need right at your disposal: copiers, computers, even a watercooler. And just think of all you could accomplish if you stopped messing around at work and actually focused. Not for your company, of course, but for you.

While it's true your little side projects could get you fired, at least you'll have something to fall back on if you do get canned.

PRO TIP

Never use work email for freelance correspondence, and save any incriminating files as "Definitely_Not_Freelance.doc."

WHERE TO LOOK FOR SECOND JOBS

- *Craigslist*
- *Monster*
- *LinkedIn*
- *Simply Hired*

Read Your Significant Other's Diary

"I never travel without my diary. One should always have something sensational to read in the train."
—Oscar Wilde, writer

It's sitting there starting at you: the small leather-bound book with a gold sash at the most recently written page. Inside it contains the unfiltered peek into your significant other's mind. It's scary, and the thought passes through your mind: *do I betray the trust I've spent months building up and read it? Or do I let this opportunity pass me by?*

Of course you know the answer: dive in headfirst. If your partner didn't want you to read it, it would be better hidden. Plus, you're dating, so you shouldn't have any secrets from each other (except for the fact that you think your partner's best friend is really hot—that can stay a secret). What the diary contains could blow your mind. Who does your significant other really want to sleep with? What does your S.O. hate most about you? What's the worst thing your S.O. thinks? Finally you'll have a chance to know everything.

Too bad all it contains is a vision of your future together, picking out furniture and baby names and some details of a family fight. The scariest thing you find out: your partner is lame.

PRO TIP

Memorize the exact position, angle, and direction
of the diary before you pick it up so you can return it
to its original position.

Pee in Public

"I gotta pee."

—*Forrest Gump*, Forrest Gump

Inevitably in life we will all find ourselves in the following predicament. We're out in public, there is no available bathroom, and we really, really have to pee. This can happen through no fault of our own. Our options are to either (1) pee our pants, or (2) find somewhere discreet to pee. Clearly the latter is the proper response.

Some find it gross or unsavory, but it's not the worst thing a person can do. It's not only convenient, but it's also the environmentally friendly way to pee. When you pee in nature, there's no wasted toilet water. Plus, if you find the right spot, you might even help hydrate a plant. So when people ask you what your carbon footprint is, tell them that while you may have three refrigerators and run the A/C with the door open, you just peed in the park, so maybe they should rethink their lifestyle.

PRO TIP

Look out to make sure nobody is around when you pee. In some states the law defines public urination as a sex offense. No bathroom emergency is worth that.

MOST POPULAR THINGS TO DRAW WITH YOUR PEE IN THE SNOW

1. Snow angels
2. Middle finger
3. Signing your name
4. Any Jackson Pollock painting

Buy Something You Don't Need

"Buying is a profound pleasure."
—Simone de Beauvoir, writer

Ever since you were a kid, people have advised, warned, and nagged you about saving money. You've been told to open a savings account, start a 401(k), think of your future, and above all else, "avoid frivolous purchases." That's all well and good if you don't want to start having fun until you retire, but what about the here and now? There's a lot to be said for living in the present.

A 70-inch flat-screen TV? A ride-on lawn mower? An indoor cloud maker? Sure, they're useless and expensive—and you don't even have a lawn to mow—but that's beside the point.

Think of all the things you've ever hesitated to buy and then make them yours. Don't even take a moment to think about it; just break out your credit card and start swiping. It doesn't even have to be something that will last a lifetime. Splurge on an expensive round of golf or an extravagant meal. The more self-indulgent, the better.

Sure, saving money can be gratifying in the future, but spending it can give you pleasure right now.

PRO TIP

Bouncing a check or overdrawing your account will put a damper on your shopping spree. Make sure you have enough money to cover your purchases.

Rock Out in the Shower

"There's no half singing in the shower.
You're either a rock star or an opera diva."
—Josh Groban, musician

Singing out loud can be fun and therapeutic, but most of us would rather die than hum a few bars in public. Luckily there's one place where everyone can sing like a rock star without feeling self-conscious: the bathroom.

You may lack the confidence to perform onstage, but you should be able to handle an audience of shampoo bottles and body wash. Invest in some waterproof speakers and cue up your favorite guilty pleasure song. You're all alone anyway, so nobody's going to judge your taste in music. Grab a loofah microphone and put on the performance of your life. Butcher the lyrics and mangle the high notes. If anybody does overhear, just ignore the bangs on the door and pleas to quiet down. A true star stops rocking for no one.

PRO TIP

Resist the urge to break into a choreographed dance in your tub.

SOUNDPROOFING YOUR SHOWER

- Close all windows
- Turn on the fan to create white noise
- Stuff towels underneath the door
- Set the water to the highest (read: loudest) setting

Unleash Your
Inner Road Rage

"Road rage is the expression of the amateur sociopath in all of us,
cured by running into a professional."
—Robert Breault, writer

On the road there are obstacles in every direction: bikers who swerve
into the street, a double-parked car that's blocking the lane, jaywalking
pedestrians. Considering you're driving something that's capable of
decapitating someone with the slightest mistake, it can be pretty stressful.
Typically you vent your frustrations by directing a small honk in the
offending pedestrian's direction or just muttering under your breath as your
hairs fall out one by one. But now the time has come to let your inner road
rage out. Lay on that horn. Scream out the window. Swerve close to hitting
the person. Feel free to even get out of your car and get in the person's face.
This is the only way drivers will ever get the voice they have for so long
been lacking. And your doctor says it's better to express yourself than to
keep your feelings bottled in. It's healthy, it's good for society, and you'll feel
great when you're done.

PRO TIP

Avoid Hells Angels
motorcyclists.

Eat Only Fast Food for a Day

"My idea of fast food is a mallard."
—Ted Nugent, musician

Expensive meals like lobster Newburg or duck confit are jaw-droppingly decadent, but sometimes you just need a good old-fashioned fast-food burger. Not only is fast food delicious, but you also just can't beat the convenience of a meal that goes from the grill to your mouth in less than five minutes.

Unfortunately fast food is about as healthy as the oil in which it's deep-fried, so it should really be only an occasional indulgence. On the other hand, you could always just blow through a year's worth of indulgences in a single day. If you can eat ten burgers a year without any ill effects, it stands to reason that you could eat the same amount in twenty-four hours. As long as you don't make it a habit, one over-the-top day won't kill you—probably.

Start yourself off slow with a doughnut and coffee, and work your way up to burgers and fries by lunchtime. Hit up all your favorite fast-food joints throughout the day, but make sure you stick solely to fast food. If it doesn't have a dollar menu, you don't want to be eating there.

PRO TIP

Hit up each fast-food venue only once to avoid judgmental fry cooks.

Turn Your Cube
Into an Office

"I was sitting in my cubicle today, and I realized ever since I started working, every single day of my life has been worse than the day before it."
—Peter Gibbons, Office Space

Waking up at the crack of dawn and battling traffic on the way to work is bad enough. Do we really have to be crammed into tiny boxes when we get there?

Four walls. Enough space for a computer and a monitor. Perhaps even a door. That's not really asking too much. But since everybody else is so satisfied with the status quo, you need to take matters into your own hands.

Rummage around for some building materials and start working on your faux office space. Track down a large, unused bulletin board to serve as a makeshift door. Layered cardboard boxes can serve as a ceiling.

To give yourself some extra storage space, duct-tape a few shelves along the walls of your new "office." Sure, it will look like crap, but at least you will be able to work in private.

PRO TIP

Don't bother clearing your construction project with HR first. It's easier to ask for forgiveness than permission.

BENEFITS TO HAVING AN OFFICE

- Nobody can look over your shoulder
- You don't have to wear headphones to listen to music
- People assume your job is important

Play with Your Child's Toys

"In every real man a child is hidden that wants to play."
—Friedrich Nietzsche, German philosopher

You see them lying there: dozens of your kid's mini hot rod cars with their supercool twisty racetrack, basically just taking up space. What a waste—especially when here you are, waiting for him to get home from preschool, feeling a little bored and unmotivated to start that next load of laundry. Time to put those toys to good use. Pick up those cars and race them across the kitchen floor. Grab those Transformers and declare war on the G.I. Joes. Dress Barbie in the outfits you totally would have loved as a ten-year-old. (Okay, maybe you still love them.) If your son or daughter happens to stumble on your play session, chances are he or she will be thrilled to join in.

Think about it: your kid's got about ninety-seven different types of toys. What's the harm in playing with one? Especially when no one's looking.

PRO TIP

Be careful not to get so carried away that your child starts questioning your commitment to the principle of sharing.

BARBIE'S REAL NAME

Barbara Millicent Roberts is the full name of the original Barbie doll.

Don't Refill the Coffeepot

"I have measured out my life with coffee spoons."
—T.S. Eliot, poet

As you trudge into the office and collapse on your desk, there is one saving grace to an otherwise miserable morning: a nice, hot cup of coffee. But once you finish topping off your mug with the last drops from the pot, you are presented with the ultimate office dilemma: to refill or not to refill.

As long as nobody's watching, the answer is obvious: bail. Once you've gotten your fill—and checked to make sure the coast is clear—nonchalantly place the pot back in the machine and saunter off. Find a secluded area to enjoy your tasty beverage before anyone realizes the pot is empty. Once you are done, head back to the kitchen and join the witch hunt to track down the culprit. In reality, you're doing your coworkers a favor by leaving the pot empty. Perhaps instead of overcaffeinated brown sludge, they'll turn to healthier options, like orange juice or soy milk.

PRO TIP

Destroy any security camera footage highlighting your lack of human decency.

PENANCE SHOULD YOU BE CAUGHT

- Wear a scarlet *C* on your shirt.
- Be forced to drink decaf for a month.
- Buy Frappuccinos for the whole office.

Get Drunk Before Noon

*"An intelligent man is sometimes forced to be drunk
to spend time with his fools."*
—Ernest Hemingway, writer

There's a universally shared belief that it is morally reprehensible to start drinking before 12:00 p.m. Most of us oblige without asking questions, but it's quite possible we're missing out on something magical as a result.

For starters, you are more in need of a drink first thing in the morning than any other time of day. A shot of tequila is at least ten times more effective at waking you up than even the strongest cup of coffee. What's more, imagine how much more enjoyable your day will be if you are already sloshed before it's even really begun.

Start your morning off right with a good old-fashioned shot of whiskey, and wash it down with your favorite microbrew. If you prefer wine, by all means crack open a bottle of your favorite vintage and sip away until noon.

This isn't about getting trashed off whatever's cheap and available; it's about indulging in your drink of choice whenever you damn well please—not when society deems it's acceptable.

PRO TIP

Enlist a drinking buddy to help you with this activity. Drinking before noon may be okay, but drinking alone before noon is the epitome of sad.

IRISH COFFEE RECIPE

6 ounces warm coffee
1.5 ounces Irish whiskey
½ ounce Baileys Irish Cream

Brew a cup of your favorite coffee, add whiskey and Baileys, and serve.

Sneak Into a
Fancy Country Club

"I don't want to belong to any club that will accept me as a member."
—Groucho Marx, actor and comedian

Country clubs are nothing more than opulent adult playgrounds where pretentious jerks gather to congratulate each other on being masters of the universe. Why would anybody want to subject themselves to such awfulness? Three things: unlimited expensive booze, teams of servants attending to your every whim, and supercool smoking jackets. Enough said.

Unfortunately you can't just walk through the door in your thrift-store pants and expect to be welcomed with open arms. You'll need to blend in. This involves copying the carefully cultivated look of a prep school student, otherwise known as yacht couture. The more self-centered you look, the better.

If all else fails, pass yourself off as a caterer. Obtain a metal cart with a white tablecloth draped over it, and swiftly wheel it past the front desk and into the belly of the yuppie beast. Now that you're in, you can play the part of the club member and have a few drinks, play a round of golf, chat up that cute employee, and generally take advantage of your ill-gotten status.

Wasn't the danger worth it?

PRO TIP

If you're sneaking across the golf green, avoid any stray balls, and try not to get any grass stains on your spotless clothes.

Take a Bookstore Book with You Into the Bookstore Bathroom

"A bookstore is one of the only pieces of evidence
we have that people are still thinking."
—Jerry Seinfeld, actor and comedian

It's a fact of nature that human beings like to read when they go to the bathroom. It's a great way to multitask and take advantage of what would otherwise be wasted time. And no place tempts you more with this than a bookstore. When you're perusing the latest new releases and suddenly you have to make your latest new release, you'll find yourself surrounded by thousands of books to choose from. Maybe you find one and maybe you start to head to the bathroom, and all of a sudden you see the sign: "Do not bring unpurchased books into the bathroom with you." It stops you for a second, and the choice is before you. Either turn back or keep walking. Just think: the bookstore is practically tempting you with the selection. Just take a quick glance around and make sure no one's watching, then march into the bathroom with determination and read to your heart's content.

PRO TIP	IT'S A NATIONAL HOLIDAY
Reserve one hand for the book and the other hand for all other bathroom-related things.	The Bathroom Readers' Institute has declared June National Bathroom Reading Month.

Stomp on Sandcastles

"And so castles made of sand fall in the sea eventually."
—*Jimi Hendrix, musician*

There's nothing so pleasant and enjoyable as crafting the perfect sandcastle—aside from stomping around and crushing one to oblivion, of course.

Stomping on sandcastles gives you all the pleasure of citywide destruction and mayhem without any of the guilt associated with destroying actual buildings. Who wouldn't want to try it? Wait until all of the families have taken their kids off the beach for the day, and have a free-for-all with the abandoned sandcastles. Pretend you are an invading monster and stomp your way from one delicate structure to the next.

As you survey the devastation, take comfort in the fact that the sandcastles were doomed from the beginning. The sea is far more destructive than you could ever be.

PRO TIP

Watch out for hidden moats and holes while you rampage. Even monsters aren't immune to broken ankles.

THE WORLD'S SANDIEST SANDCASTLE

In 2017 a group of artists constructed the world's largest sandcastle in Duisburg, Germany. It stood fifty-four feet, nine inches high, and used 168 trucks of sand.

Use the TV as a Babysitter

"When I got my first television set, I stopped caring so much about having close relationships."
—Andy Warhol, artist

You know that mom at playgroup who insists her children have never watched a second of television? She's a pain in the ass and not to be trusted.

Every time your kids start to drive you crazy, you fantasize about sitting them in front of the TV and escaping for a little "me time"—even if that just means drawing a bubble bath for yourself. Well, who says you can't?

These days television shows like *Sesame Street* and *Ready Jet Go!* are both entertaining and educational for young minds. Besides, a couple of hours of TV never hurt anyone. You turned out just fine, right? Block out the inappropriate channels so your kids don't accidentally stumble across something scary or graphic. Better yet, pop in a Disney movie or two or three, and keep them entertained for hours.

PRO TIP

Resurrect the baby monitor so you can still keep a watchful eye on them if they start to fight or get into something they shouldn't.

HOW DO YOU GET TO *SESAME STREET*?

The quintessential children's television program *Sesame Street*, which debuted in 1969, can be seen in more than 140 countries.

Hire a Hot Pool Cleaner for Your Tub

"I've been dating younger men since my twenties. When I was twenty-nine, I dated someone twenty-one... younger men are just more fun. I like their energy."
—Dana Delany, actress

If television has taught us anything, it's that there is nothing better than lounging on a patio chair while a scantily clad twenty-something cleans your pool. If only you had a pool of your own—and disposable income—you could see for yourself.

Well, let's think about exactly what makes a pool a pool. If you define it as simply a large container filled with water, well then, by golly, you've got everything you need to live out your fantasy sitting in your bathroom. You just happen to call it a bathtub. Track down your local pool-cleaning service and say you have a special job for the right candidate. Since your "pool" is really dirty and requires lots of cleaning, explain that you need someone who is in shape and up to the task. When your temporary servant arrives, don't bother trying to pass your tub off as a pool. Just pull up a chair, pour yourself a margarita, and tell your cleaner to get to work...but not to rush through it.

PRO TIP

Dirty the tub before the cleaner arrives so you have longer to admire the view.

Bake an Entire Cake and Eat Just the Frosting

"Y'all can have your cake but that ain't $#%@ without the frosting."
—Sam Adams, musician

Let's face it: everybody eats cake for the sugary, creamy frosting on top. Without it, cake's no better than a breakfast muffin. In fact, if tradition didn't insist otherwise, you'd reverse the cake-to-icing ratio right around. If you're really being honest, the truth is that you'd skip the cake altogether and just go for a delicious helping of the gooey florets and "Happy Birthday" letters adorned on top.

It's time to give in to the decadence and finally eat cake the way you like it. Whether you're a fan of cake mixes or prefer to bake from scratch, whip up a cake to use as your frosting platform. Don't get too picky because the icing is where the real work comes in. Use tubes, sprinkles, and plenty of frosting tubs; spread on the sugary goodness thick like a Van Gogh. Feel free to be thorough or sloppy in your craft; just make sure you're generous in your adornments.

When your masterpiece is done, grab a fork and skim off as much as you can, gathering only a few crumbs of the layer below. The reward is like, well, icing on the cake.

PRO TIP
....
To prevent nausea or a severe
sugar crash, don't attempt
this on an empty stomach.

Refuse to Share

"There are only two things a child will share willingly—communicable diseases and his mother's age."
—Dr. Benjamin Spock, physician

It's easy to remember the kindergarten lessons that stick with you throughout life. Look both ways before crossing the street, don't bite people you don't like, and above all, share with others. But let's be honest: sometimes you just don't want to share a damn thing.

Lucky for you, it's not kindergarten anymore, so you don't have to. Of course it's the nice, polite thing to do, but everyone deserves a day once in a while where they keep everything to themselves. So go ahead and hog everything you want, from your favorite orange highlighter to your french fries at lunch.

Don't feel bad about it either—it would be absurd to think that everyone else shares everything all the time. And if people do try to make you feel bad about not sharing, just let out a big sneeze and say, "Sorry, I'm coming down with something. What were you saying?" Chances are they'll leave you alone.

PRO TIP

Avoid ordering movie popcorn on days where you don't plan to share. Otherwise you could start a riot.

KEEP THESE ITEMS TO YOURSELF

- Used Kleenex
- Ice cream cones
- Nasal spray
- Religious views

Create a Supersecret Candy Stash

"Research tells us fourteen out of any ten individuals like chocolate."
—Sandra Boynton, writer and cartoonist

There are two certainties when stocking an office candy drawer: (1) you will gain five pounds the first month, and (2) your coworkers will flock to the sound of rustling wrappers like moths to a flame. Enter the double-secret candy stash; sharing is for suckers.

Just because you want an afternoon snack does not mean you should have to feed your entire office. If your coworkers like candy so much, they can very well buy their own. Besides, the last thing your hyperactive cubemate needs is more sugar.

First and foremost, create a decoy candy drawer with mints and licorice to draw attention away from your real stash. Now you need to find a hiding place for your real stash. Storing your sweets in an unlocked drawer is simply out of the question. That's the first place people would look. Instead, try more creative hiding places like a hollowed-out dictionary or your monthly expense reports binder.

PRO TIP

Dispose of stray wrappers immediately after consumption so you don't arouse suspicion.

BEST CANDY HIDING PLACES

- Underneath a loose floorboard
- Bucket labeled "Not Candy"
- Inside a box of granola bars

Steal Candy from a Baby

"A lot of people like lollipops. I don't like lollipops. To me, a lollipop is hard candy plus garbage. I don't need a handle. Just give me the candy."
—Demetri Martin, comedian

It's late in the afternoon, and an insatiable sugar craving hits. Alas, your coworkers depleted your secret candy drawer months ago. Lucky for you, it's Bring Your Child to Work Day.

Despite what you may have heard, taking candy from babies is not easy. What they lack in physical strength and intelligence, they make up for in blood-curdling screaming ability. Also, their inherent cuteness deters all but the most hardened candy thieves. But you're hungry, dammit. Employ a clever distraction to eliminate Mom and isolate the infant. Phone in a bomb threat, have her car towed, whatever it takes. Now, with lightning-fast speed and agility, approach the target and liberate the candy. Before the baby realizes what hit it, quietly return to your desk and consume the evidence.

There will be crying, but you must not give in to your inevitable feelings of guilt. Besides, if you chose your target wisely, it will be months before it develops the cognitive skills necessary to implicate you in the crime.

PRO TIP

Check the office for baby monitors and nanny cams. Perfect your balloon-animal-making skills to distract the target.

EASIER WAYS TO GET CANDY

- Get a haircut
- Be a good boy or girl at the doctor
- Visit your grandmother

Have an
Upside-Down Dinner

"Life is uncertain. Eat dessert first."
—Ernestine Ulmer, writer

Dessert is obviously the best part of any meal, yet over and over again we gorge ourselves on mediocre dinner fare until there's no room left for sweets. And each time we do that, our inner child dies a little inside. The solution is as elegant as it is simple: eat dessert first.

There are some things that just need to happen in order—like thinking of an excuse before you call in sick to work. But the time frame of eating dessert simply does not fall into that category. It's not like coating your stomach with steak will prevent the cheesecake from making you fat. So you might as well give in to your sweet tooth.

When your waiter gets to the table, kindly ask to see the dessert menu before you even look at the dinner options. Indulge yourself with ice cream, fruit tarts, French pastries, and anything else that catches your eye.

Once you are filled to capacity, take a moment to see if you have room for dinner. You might not even need to bother.

PRO TIP

Finish all the pie that's on your plate, or else you won't get any chicken.

OTHER UPSIDE-DOWN ADVENTURES

- Workweek (take Monday/ Tuesday off)
- Road trip (start complaining, then get in the car)
- Fight (apologize first, then start punching)

Take Advantage of Your Lunch Break

"Ask not what you can do for your country. Ask what's for lunch."
—Orson Welles, actor and director

This may not come as a surprise, but your lunch hour is valuable time that should be used for your benefit, not as an opportunity to finish collating spreadsheets or to listen to the twenty-five neglected voice mails on your work phone. Despite that, nearly half of all employees take fewer than thirty minutes to eat their lunch each day, and many do so while working at their desks. So today you're going to damn The Man and take back what is rightfully yours.

When the clock strikes noon, get the hell out of Dodge and don't look back. Enjoy a hot meal at a nice restaurant, or just take a siesta on a park bench. You could even use the time to sneak in a few sets at the gym or run a few errands.

Whatever you do with your time, it will be infinitely better than staring at a computer screen.

PRO TIP

Check your watch before you leave so you keep it to about an hour.

OTHER THINGS TO RECLAIM

- Coffee breaks
- Watercooler chats
- Half-day Fridays

Sleep for Twenty-Four Hours

"There is only one thing people like that is good for them:
a good night's sleep."
—Edgar Watson Howe, editor

These days nobody gets enough sleep. Most people are lucky if they snooze six hours a night, and plenty get by with even less. While it's impossible to make up for all that lost slumber in a single day, you can certainly make a dent.

Spending an entire twenty-four hours in bed might seem like a waste of time, but what else would you be doing with that time? Unlike going to the movies, paying bills, or driving to the beach, sleeping all day requires no money and burns zero fossil fuels. It's good for the environment and the soul.

This is going to be the single laziest, most relaxing day of your life, so make sure you have plenty of pillows, warm blankets, and comfortable pajamas. Do your best to put all of your responsibilities out of your mind and focus on the task at hand—pure, unadulterated sleep.

PRO TIP

If you are a light sleeper, keep a fan running nearby to create white noise and block out any interruptions.

BEST SLEEP AIDS

- Morgan Freeman recordings
- Civil War documentaries
- *War and Peace*

Take the Largest Slice of Pizza

"There's no better feeling in the world than a warm pizza box on your lap."
—Kevin James, actor

No matter how hard you try, it's physically impossible to carve a pizza into nice, even slices. There's always going to be a few baby slices dwarfed by their mammoth counterparts.

Proper etiquette suggests you settle for the puny slices and offer up the more substantial pieces to your hungry guests, but why should you suffer just because your friends are too cheap to buy their own pie? It's your pizza, and you should get the biggest piece.

When you cut the pie, make sure you serve yourself first and head straight for the biggest slice. If you are feeling particularly greedy, you can pull a Garfield and cut a small sliver for your guests and take the rest of the pie for yourself. You may have to deal with a few dirty looks and some irritated grumbling, but at least you won't be hungry.

PRO TIP

If you are worried about losing friends, cut the pizza away from prying eyes so your greediness won't be as obvious.

HARDEST FOODS TO SHARE

- Sandwiches
- Soups
- All restaurant desserts

Stand Up Your Ex

"Friendship often ends in love; but love in friendship—never."
—Charles Caleb Colton, writer

After a painful breakup that left you eating takeout alone and routinely polishing off a pint of Ben & Jerry's in a single sitting, it's safe to say you hit a low point. So you got dumped. And it sucked. It happens to everyone. Now it's time to get the revenge you deserve.

Whether it's been three years or three months since you last saw your ex, reach out by sending an innocuous text or email. Keep it light. Insist you'd like to make good on that "let's be friends" one-liner your ex so brilliantly declared the last time you were together. Invite your ex to a very fancy, very public restaurant where you're bound to see people both of you know. Put the reservation under your name, and confirm the date and time with your ex. Then go see a movie across town instead. Revenge may be sweet, but humiliation is sweeter.

PRO TIP

Turn your phone off during the movie so you can successfully ignore the multiple phone calls and text messages your ex is bound to leave you.

THE FIVE STAGES OF BEING STOOD UP

1. "Oh look, I'm the first one here!"
2. "They must be running late."
3. "It's probably car trouble—I'll try calling."
4. "No answer on the phone—that's strange."
5. "Whatever. I prefer eating alone anyway."

Pay for a Parking Ticket in Pennies

"You know, somebody actually complimented me on my driving today. They left a little note on the windscreen; it said 'Parking Fine.'"
—Tommy Cooper, comedian

There's no worse feeling than getting a parking ticket. Suddenly that coffee you ran in for without paying the meter costs five times as much, and it feels like everyone in the whole world is against you. So give it right back to them: instead of cutting a check like you're expected to do, take the opportunity to empty out your piggy bank—and pay the ticket in pennies.

It's legal tender—they have to take it. So have some fun with it and make it a game. The more coins you use to equal the amount of the ticket, the better. If you have only quarters or dimes, find a way to exchange them for pennies. If they're going to take your money, you're going to take their time.

Drop off the change and turn on your heel. There's no need to stay to make sure it's all there—they have your contact information if they need to get in touch.

PRO TIP

Do your research before pulling this stunt. Find out if there's a law against being a jerk or else prepare to be arrested.

OTHER PAYMENT OPTIONS

- IOU (it is better than money)
- Pay in trade
- Marbles—lots of marbles

Perfect Your Cannonball

"One never dives into the water to save a drowning man more eagerly than when there are others present who dare not take the risk."
—Friedrich Nietzsche, German philosopher

There's a reason pool decks are made of waterproof surfaces: they're going to get wet. So if you're on a pool deck, you run the risk of getting wet too. Why not drive that point home by practicing your cannonball in a pool lined with sunbathers? You did it when you were younger. It was always a hit at pool parties when you were a preteen. It's time to relive your glory days by participating in and winning a cannonball competition—where the only competitor is yourself.

Tanning doesn't require water; swimming does. So if you happen to attempt the biggest splash-producing jump in the history of pool entries, it's because you didn't have a choice. If the tanners are afraid to get wet, they should go tan somewhere where the splash can't reach them—like in a tanning bed.

PRO TIP

Before taking the plunge, find out how long you can hold your breath. Then stay underwater for as long as possible after cannonballing into the pool so that people's anger has a few more seconds to dissipate.

OTHER POOL ACTIVITIES TO GET PEOPLE WET

- Jackknife into the pool
- Water guns
- Duck, duck, goose (with water)
- Water balloons

Get Free Refills All Night

"Let's all go to the lobby to get ourselves a treat!"
—1953 animated movie theater snack bar advertisement

Dinner and a movie is America's favorite date night. The only problem? A romantic meal and two tickets to the latest blockbuster can easily set you back fifty bucks. It's tempting to lower the price tag by scrimping on dinner or trading the big screen for Netflix at home, but where's the fun in that? Instead of cutting back, squeeze every penny you can out of the restaurant and the movie theater concession stand: exploit the free-refill policy. Look for menu items described as "unlimited," "bottomless," or "endless." You might not think you can make a meal out of bottomless soft drinks and unlimited breadsticks, but you would be wrong. At the movies, splurge for the large popcorn and soda. Remember that you're spending money to save money. After five or six refills, those snacks will have paid for themselves.

PRO TIP

Eat a light breakfast and lunch. You don't want to miss out on any delicious bread-sticks, soft drinks, or popcorn because you overdid it on your morning cereal.

MAKING THE MOST OF THE REFILL

Sneak a resealable bag and an empty cup into the movie theater. As soon as you sit down, transfer your snacks to the empty containers and give them to your date. Refill the original packages. Repeat. And repeat again.

Participate in Obnoxious PDA

"A kiss is a lovely trick designed by nature to stop speech when words become superfluous."
—Ingrid Bergman, actress

When it comes to public displays of affection, there are a few general rules. Be as discreet as possible, keep your hands where we can see them, and please—for the love of God—no tongue. Good thing you care as much about decorum as you do about the mating habits of African fruit flies. Nobody has the right to tell you when, or how far, you can shove your tongue down your partner's throat. If they don't like it, they can find another bench to sit on.

Throw caution to the wind and hug, kiss, grope, and nuzzle your significant other to your heart's content. Not enough seats at the restaurant? Just sit on your partner's lap. No space on the subway? Just hug each other as close as possible. If you are obnoxious enough, the rest of the world may just give you some privacy for a change.

PRO TIP

Keep it PG-13. You want to be annoying, not wind up in prison.

MOST OFFENSIVE FORMS OF PDA

- Hands in each other's back pockets
- Playing footsie
- Incessant baby talk

Commandeer Control
of the TV Remote

"Men definitely hit the remote more than women.
Men don't care what's on TV, men only care what else is on TV.
Women want to see what the show is before they change the
channel, because men hunt and women nest."
—*Jerry Seinfeld*, Seinfeld

There's a lot of crap on TV, and frankly your family's tastes aren't cutting it. Flipping between *The Big Bang Theory*, *Grey's Anatomy*, and CNN isn't providing the kind of consistency of entertainment that you're hoping to zone out to right now. Plus, they're watching too many commercials and missing too much of the key action sequences on each of the three shows you're trying to watch simultaneously. They've shown they're not capable of handling the responsibility of holding the TV remote.

The time has come to take control of the operation. Snag the remote and start captaining the ship. Your choice in entertainment is better than anyone else's in the room, and your ability to accurately estimate commercial break times is unparalleled. Plus, you want to watch what you want to watch. It's that simple. The time for politely deferring to your family is over. Stage a coup and take over the TV remote throne.

PRO TIP

Try to have spare batteries nearby in case an
ensuing fight results in the batteries being
ejected from the remote.

Buy Costume Jewelry and Pass It Off as the Real Thing

"Maybe I'm paranoid, but in this day and age, I don't want something around my neck that's worth more than my head."
—Rita Rudner, comedian

How many times have you gazed longingly at someone else's jewelry and thought, *If only I could afford that?* Sadly most of us don't have a sugar daddy or sugar mama to buy us pretty things, but don't let that stop you from having beautiful jewelry.

Costume jewelry was invented for just this purpose. Although costume jewelry is often tacky and over the top, it's perfectly possible to find pieces that not only look gorgeous but could also pass for the real thing. So whether you've got your eye on a gold-plated watch or a set of pearls, find what you want, buy it, and wear it with pride.

People wear costume jewelry every day to all kinds of functions, so there's nothing to be embarrassed about. Chances are that once you've made and flaunted your purchases, you'll be the one people want to emulate.

PRO TIP

When you're shopping, consulting a jeweler is the best way to make good purchases without breaking the bank.

THE ORIGIN OF FAUX FASHION

Costume jewelry was created in the 1930s as a cheap, disposable accessory meant to compliment a specific outfit.

Leave the Dishes
for Tomorrow

"Best way to get rid of kitchen odors: eat out."
—Phyllis Diller, comedian

After slaving away to make dinner yet again, you've enjoyed a leisurely meal complete with an overindulgence in your favorite adult beverage. You clear the table post-feast, only to be abruptly reminded of the complete and utter mess lurking in your kitchen.

Instead of breaking down and reaching for the closest sponge to attack that glaring mound of dirty dishes, just turn around and walk away. Surely your best stainless steel pot won't be ruined by an extra twenty-four hours of mashed potato residue. Nor will that once-delicious-but-now-disgusting-looking caramelized barbecue sauce leave a permanent scar on your grandmother's frying pan.

It's been a long day, so treat yourself to a mini marathon of ESPN programming, or pull out the latest issue of *US Weekly* that's stashed in your nightstand. You've done enough dishes in your life to know that sometimes the mess can just wait. And anyway, it's your significant other's turn to wash the dishes, isn't it?

PRO TIP

Turn off the kitchen lights to make the mess disappear.

HOW TO PERMANENTLY ESCAPE DISH DUTY

- Hire a maid
- Use only paper plates
- Eat nothing but TV dinners

Steal Veggies from the Community Garden

"I have a rock garden. Last week three of them died."
—Richard Diran, writer

As you watch your neighbors toil and putter in the soil, you can't help but wonder why they spend so much time in the community garden—that is, until they let you taste one of their fresh summer tomatoes and every corner of your mouth explodes with glee. It's too late to start growing your own produce, but it's never too late to grub off theirs.

Most community gardens are practically overflowing with veggies—far too many for the participating gardeners to consume. If you don't grab some now, they'll sit on the vine and rot. And you can't let that happen. Better start harvesting.

Wait for the dead of night and hop over the rickety fence surrounding the garden. Take your pick of the plumpest carrots, the juiciest tomatoes, and the spiciest hot peppers. Once you've gathered all your arms can carry, flee to a secluded area to eat the evidence.

PRO TIP

Bring a neighborhood cat along to use as a patsy.

EASIEST FOOD TO STEAL UNNOTICED

- Berries
- Tomatoes
- Peppers

Wear Sexy Lingerie Under Jeans and a T-Shirt

"I wear women's leggings under my clothes, but no lingerie."
—Dennis Rodman, basketball player

When you pull on a pair of jeans in the morning, the obvious next step is to throw on the nearest T-shirt and slide into a pair of sneakers. It's comfortable and all, but unless you're Brooke Shields circa 1980, it doesn't exactly signal sex appeal. Besides, most of us prefer to have something between ourselves and our Calvins.

Well, there's a quick way to keep the outfit but add a little punch. Every woman has them: fancy undies that were bought as a special set for a special night but that don't get much regular use. And let's face it: a little fabric can cost a pretty penny. You paid good money and you might as well get something out of it. The next time you pull on a casual outfit, skip the faded cotton underwear and reach for your raciest, laciest lingerie. Sure, you probably bought those skivvies because you wanted them to be seen, but walking around with a little hidden secret makes the sexiest lingerie even sexier.

PRO TIP

Be unexpected but practical: don't swap out your underwear on a day you're playing dodgeball or raking the yard. After all, you want that lingerie looking fresh for the next time it's worn after hours.

Grab a Pint of Ice Cream and Crawl Into Bed

"Without ice cream, there would be darkness and chaos."
—Don Kardong, athlete

One of life's greatest pleasures is crawling into a comfortable bed at the end of the day. This feeling of satisfaction is rivaled only by the joy of eating ice cream.

Unfortunately we all know the rules for both of these experiences. You're not supposed to eat in bed. You're supposed to have only one serving of ice cream, and you're supposed to eat it out of a bowl. Well, you're an adult now and there's no one to enforce those silly rules. Pop open a fresh pint of your favorite Ben & Jerry's (as long as it's not low-fat or frozen yogurt) and walk straight out of the kitchen, pausing only to grab a spoon. Tonight you're eating directly out of the pint, and you're not standing up at the kitchen sink either. You're going to see what happens when the luxury of whole milk, cane sugar, and Tahitian vanilla beans combines with the comfort of your very own bed. So bundle up in your fluffiest down comforter and lean back on a stack of pillows. You're taking dessert to a whole new level of decadence.

PRO TIP

Savor the experience. The only thing that can ruin it is rushing through your pint and giving yourself a Level One brain freeze.

Blow Your Savings on the Lottery

"I've done the calculation, and your chances of winning the lottery are identical whether you play or not."
—Fran Lebowitz, writer

There are literally dozens of ways to invest your money. You can buy bonds, stick your money in a CD, open an IRA, or simply stuff it in a mattress. Sadly, regardless of which method you choose, it'll be years before you see any significant returns.

If you want instant gratification, there's only one thing to do: invest in the lottery.

While it's true the odds of winning the lottery with a single ticket are minuscule, this is precisely why you have to buy thousands of them. Besides, it's not really that much worse than playing the stock market. The only difference is that with the lottery, you actually know where your money is going.

Cash out your savings account and bring your stacks of cash straight to the local convenience store. Diversify your investment by buying local, state, and national lottery tickets as well as a few scratch-offs for good measure. Rather than brainstorming thousands of meaningful number combinations, it's best to generate them randomly at the store. That way you'll be able to blame the cashier if all your numbers miss.

PRO TIP

Buy your ticket at the location of the last winner.
Clearly it's lucky.

Stay in Bed All Day

"You can't teach people to be lazy—either they have it or they don't."
—*Dagwood Bumstead*, Blondie

As sunlight slowly creeps its way through the curtains, you think through all of the possible ways to spend this beautiful day. You could head to the beach, go for a nice bike ride, or putter around in the garden. Then again, who says you have to do anything at all?

It may be fun to go frolicking out in the warm rays of the sun, but it can be just as gratifying to tell that burning ball of fire to bugger off while you watch cartoons. Sure, you could wait for a rainy day to sit around in your underwear, but complete and utter sloth is infinitely more satisfying when there are actually better things to do.

So unplug the alarm, wrap yourself in an extra blanket, grab a bag of chips, and see if you can make it through the entire day without leaving your bed. If you get bored, set important goals for your afternoon, like watching every episode of *Arrested Development* or beating every level of Angry Birds.

PRO TIP

Add at least seven movies to
your Netflix list.

Buy an Entire Row of Seats for Your Flight

"A hundred years ago, it could take you the better part of a year to get from New York to California, whereas today, because of equipment problems at O'Hare, you can't get there at all."

—Dave Barry, humorist

Before you book your next flight, imagine that the doors to the plane are just about to close, and your entire row is somehow still empty. Then imagine your disappointment as two passengers the size of elephants plunk down on either side of you.

While you can't remove annoying fellow passengers through sheer force of will, you can make sure they never have the chance to exist. The next time you have a long flight, go ahead and splurge—buy the entire row of seats.

That's right, the entire row. And milk that luxury for all it's worth. Read a book with your back against the window and your legs across the entire row. Pack some noodle salads and watermelon, and set up a picnic on the two spares. Curl up on all three and take a nap.

And if some poor soul squeezed into the center seat behind you asks to take one of yours, have a ready response. "I paid for these," you can say, "and they're all mine."

PRO TIP

Be sure to buckle up. You don't want turbulence raining on your luxury parade.

Drink Ten Cups of Coffee

"Coffee is a way of stealing time that should by rights
belong to your older self."
—Terry Pratchett, writer

When you've been drinking coffee as long as you have, the body builds up a resistance to the caffeine. Sometimes that one cup in the morning just doesn't do it. Sometimes even the second cup doesn't do it. Sometimes the third, fourth, and fifth cups don't even get the job done. So screw it—just drink ten cups of coffee.

It's time you show your body who's boss. If you want to wake up, dammit, it's gonna happen. And if your body doesn't respond to the first five cups of coffee, well, body, we'll just see who wins this battle of wills. The coffee machine at work is free, and you're not going anywhere. You've got all day. And now that you've had ten cups of coffee, all night too. And all of the next day as well. You may end up with a splitting headache and crash all at once, but at least you woke yourself up when you needed to.

PRO TIP

Have enough gum to cover the post-bender coffee breath.

A NATION OF ADDICTS

The average person in the United States consumes 3.1 cups of coffee per day.

Go Skinny-Dipping

"Only when the tide goes out do you discover who's been swimming naked."
—Warren Buffett, investor

After a while every day starts to feel depressingly similar to the one before. You wake up, go to work, come home, make dinner, watch TV, and go to bed. What you wouldn't give for a little spontaneity! Luckily you don't have to sell all your worldly possessions and go backpacking around Europe to shake things up. Something as simple as taking a quick dip in your outdoor pool could be all you need—naked, of course.

The average bathing suit is uncomfortable, is restrictive, and leaves almost nothing to the imagination anyway. Pick a spot for your risqué swimming session—local pond, nearby beach, neighborhood pool—and head out. You don't need to bring much along, just a towel and a sense of adventure.

When you get to the water, there's nothing left to do but strip down and dive in. Swim a few laps in your birthday suit and enjoy the cool water against your skin before you hop out and towel off. Hopefully nobody saw you, but even if they did, that's half the fun.

PRO TIP

If you are self-conscious about your body, jump into the water first and then take off your clothes.

RULES FOR SKINNY-DIPPING

1. Strip or go home. No free shows.
2. Underwear doesn't count.
3. No pointing, no laughing, no cameras.

Buy Illegal Fireworks

"The Fourth of July combines the two things Americans love most in one day: alcohol and explosives."
—David Letterman, talk show host

It's the anniversary of our great nation, and what better way to celebrate than by blowing up a small portion of it?

Sure, fireworks may be illegal in many states, but so are speeding and jaywalking and downloading pirated music. Police have bigger things to worry about than a few cherry bombs. Besides, you'd be disgracing our Founding Fathers if you didn't honor their memory with a proper pyrotechnics display.

Head to your local fireworks emporium and check out the section reserved for the more "patriotic" customers (usually located in a back room). Forget lame sparklers and noisemakers; you're looking for bottle rockets, Roman candles, and M-80s. Once you've gathered enough artillery to level a small village, you should be able to put on a first-rate fireworks show—or at least blow up a few garbage cans.

PRO TIP

Enlist local miscreants to instruct you on proper demolition protocol.

HOMEMADE TENNIS BALL BOMB

Cut a hole in a tennis ball and stuff it with the heads removed from "strike anywhere" matches. Cover the hole with tape and throw the ball against a hard surface. Run.

Go to a Nude Beach with Clothes On

"Clothes make the man. Naked people have
little or no influence on society."
—Mark Twain, writer

The first time you hear about nude beaches is probably sometime in early adolescence, and if you're like most people, you have overactive hormones that make it clear this is a place you should visit. Not to break free from the shackles of society's norms, but just to get a glimpse of the full, naked body in all its beautiful glory.

Now that you're old and out of shape, the thought of being on a nude beach might frighten you more than entice you. There's a fear that fellow nudists would pass judgment on your hairy, flabby, nutritionless torso. So rather than subject yourself to the type of shallow judgments that you would certainly have if you saw your naked self, get the best of both worlds.

Throw on your swim trunks, dab some sunscreen on your nose, and have at it. Nude beaches allow patrons to be nude. They don't require it.

PRO TIP

Wear dark or reflective sunglasses. Wandering eyes will warrant at best a chuckle and at worst a slap in the face.

QUESTIONS NOT TO ASK AT A NUDE BEACH

- "How's it hanging?"
- "Can you hold these for a second?"
- "How much longer will it be?"

Skip Work and Go to the Beach

"Life moves pretty fast. If you don't stop and look around once in a while, you could miss it."
—*Ferris Bueller,* Ferris Bueller's Day Off

You wake up to a beautiful day. You are within driving distance of a beautiful body of water, beside which lie beautiful bodies basking in the sun. You long to be one of them. But you are due at work in an hour. Accounting is expecting you. The choice is yours: finance—or fun?

Follow your gut—and call in sick to work. You know the drill: You have the flu; you ate bad Chinese food last night; you've developed a sudden allergy to shellfish.

The only accounting you're going to do today involves beach chairs, bikinis, and booze. Type the location of the nearest ocean, river, lake, or country club pool into your GPS. Load up your transport with all of the sinner's accoutrements: towels, umbrella, ghetto blaster, sexy novels, KFC bucket, cooler full of Beach-Proof Margaritas. Slip into the skimpiest bathing suit you own. Don a sun hat or baseball cap. And don't forget a killer pair of sunglasses. You look good. You know you do. Now go play hooky.

PRO TIP

Use plenty of sunscreen. You can explain away a little color, but a bright red sunburn will arouse unwelcome suspicion.

Score a Ride on a Stranger's Boat

"You have to be careful on the deck because of the 'hatches,' which are holes placed around a sailboat at random to increase the insurance rates."
—Dave Barry, humorist

You've been cooped up indoors for what seems like an eternity and are eager to make the most of the summer season. Unfortunately you still don't know anyone who owns a boat. This time around, though, you're not going to let that stop you.

Grab a friend (safety first!) and take a stroll down to the local pier, taking note of good sailing prospects—like that friendly-looking portly gentleman who keeps eyeing you from his sailboat or the cougar who won't stop giving you a "come hither" look. After playing coy for a few minutes, walk over and flirt it up—chances are you'll be onboard in no time. That's not to say you won't be able to find a boat buddy closer to your own age group, but boats equal money, so don't be surprised if you find yourself flirting with the newest president of AARP. Don't feel bad about it either— you get an afternoon on a boat, and the boat buddy gets an ego boost. Everybody wins!

PRO TIP

Allowing your sailing companion to rub sunscreen on you will result in both brownie points and UV protection.

Watch the Game at Work

"We are inclined to think that if we watch a football game
or a baseball game, we have taken part in it."
—John F. Kennedy, US president

Many important sporting events take place during the day. The Chicago Cubs famously play day games most of the week. The first two rounds of the NCAA Tournament take place on weekdays. Many college football bowls are during the day as well. Watching these games is certainly better than working, so open a new Google Chrome window and watch some sporty ball at work.

Depending on your workplace, this might be dangerous or it might be tolerated but frowned upon. Either way you'll have to keep a low profile. Bring in a pair of earphones so as not to disturb those near you. Also, you should practice not cheering during a game a few times before trying it at work. But once it's safe, it's a great way to be able to enjoy the time you spend at work. Plus, you'll have all the latest sports news to disseminate to your officemates. Your cool factor just increased by one. Many games available on network websites offer the "Boss Button."

PRO TIP

If you click the "Boss Button," the screen immediately changes to a workflow chart or something else that looks like real work. Use it when your boss comes by.

INAPPROPRIATE AT-WORK SPORTS GAME BEHAVIOR

- Tailgating
- Body paint
- Foam fingers
- Audible cheering
- Doing the wave
- Drinking

Hire a Chauffeur to Ferry Your Kids Around

*"Children aren't happy without something to ignore,
and that's what parents were created for."*
—Ogden Nash, humorist

Kids are the source of much joy and pride, but let's be honest: the little suckers are demanding. Between driving them to the mall, movies, and friends' houses, when are you supposed to have time for yourself? That's why you should hire someone to do it for you.

This is especially important once they hit the age where they're embarrassed to be seen with you. It doesn't matter how cool you are (or how cool you once were—you can try to convince them of that, but they'll never believe you). They'll insist you drop them off around the corner so their friends don't have to see your minivan or "This Car Climbed Mount Washington" bumper sticker.

All they need is a ride—they don't care who they get it from. So hire a chauffeur and take a few minutes to yourself.

PRO TIP

Conduct an extensive background check on your chauffeur. These are your kids, after all. You can't trust them with just anyone.

WHAT TO DO WITH ALL OF YOUR NEW FREE TIME

- Sleep
- Take up a new hobby
- Catch up on your TV shows
- Sleep some more
- Think of other ways to pawn your kids off on other people

Purposely Fart at Important Life Moments

"My philosophy of dating is to just fart right away."
—Jenny McCarthy, actress and model

Let's face it: you're onstage doing something serious and everyone is looking at you. Maybe it's your bar mitzvah or your graduation, or you're getting married. Who really cares? Does it really matter? Are you going to take this moment that seriously?

Hell no, you're not. Because you're in a tuxedo. And nobody is expecting it. And you're a comedy genius, which means you realize that there is nothing funnier than a well-timed, unexpected, loud and unignorable fart to shake things up. That's why you ate a can of beans an hour earlier—to prepare for this moment. And when it comes, dear lord, will it be glorious. Hire a videographer and instruct her to get reaction shots of your family. It will be the best investment of your life. This video may be the launching pad for your Internet fame, and you'll want to be able to show your kids the tape one day.

PRO TIP

Warn your elderly family members of what is to come. You don't want anyone to faint from shock.

WAYS TO MAKE IT UP TO THOSE YOU OFFENDED

- Apology cards
- Flowers
- Free whoopie cushions
- Coupon book for one free punch in the face

Fake Sick to Get Waited Upon

"The secret of life is honesty and fair dealing.
If you can fake that, you've got it made."
—Groucho Marx, actor and comedian

Being moderately sick isn't the worst thing in the world. You get to miss work, you can stay in bed all day watching TV, and most importantly, people call to check on you and see if you're okay. Some may even cook you tomato soup and wait on you hand and foot. Alas, you're as fit as a fiddle and completely undeserving of any special care today. It sure would be nice to get treated like royalty, though. Well, like they always say, when in doubt, fake it.

All you have to do is force a few sickly coughs, lick your palms so they're nice and clammy, and put on your best "woe is me" face. If you live with someone, help should arrive shortly. If not, you might need to send some text messages. "Feeling sick, can't talk, very feverish" should get the point across. Suddenly an outpouring of concern is headed your way.

Take full advantage of your crew of well-wishers, and send them out to get you everything from chicken soup and ginger ale to gossip magazines and DVDs. They won't mind as long as it helps you along to a speedy recovery. Just make sure not to give away your ruse, or your lackeys might just give you something to feel sick about.

PRO TIP

If anyone is taking your temperature, have a heat lamp nearby to get that temperature into the fever range.

Memorial Day BBQ Hop

*"If you really want to make a friend, go to someone's house
and eat with him…the people who give you their food
give you their heart."*
—Cesar Chavez, union activist

Follow the smell of smoke and burgers, and hop from one backyard BBQ
bash to the next. So what if you weren't invited? Everyone will assume
you're a friend of someone else anyway.

Explore a variety of pasta salad preparations while seamlessly blending
in with other Memorial Day revelers. As soon as the opportunity presents
itself, challenge someone to a game of bag toss, bocce, or some other
backyard game. Make a friend. Establish your story. If you're looking
chummy with just one person, everyone will think they're the one who
invited you.

Keep a six-pack handy so it looks less suspicious when you wander in.
Everyone likes beer, right? Don't forget to replenish the stash before you're
on to the next stop.

Don't let anyone know that you're crashing the party.

PRO TIP

Always have a backstory
handy so you don't get found
out. This works best if you're
operating alone.

Communicate
Solely in Expletives

"Life is a four-letter word."
—Lenny Bruce, comedian

When we're in a rage, nothing feels better than to unleash a barrage of four-letter words on the offender. It's therapeutic, nonviolent, and generally quite fun. It's a shame we reserve such eloquent prose solely for our most frustrating moments.

The thing is those swears and vulgarities are so fun to say. It'd really make more sense to talk that way all the time in order to get your fill. Today start your day off with some %$#@ing coffee, hop on the @#&% %$!#ing train, and attend your morning meeting with that ^#& %@!&ing son of a !@^#. Maybe later you and your friends will #@!$ like $#&ing &%^#!@s, just like in the good old days.

Don't be bashful; use your expletives loud and proud, and if anyone has a problem with it, then they can !$#% off.

PRO TIP

The caveat to using profane language is in the presence of children. Parents get really @%&#ing mad about that.

BEST G-RATED CURSES

- "Dagnabbit!"
- "Oh, fruitcake!"
- "Blast and tarnation!"
- "Sweet swirling onion rings!"

Index